COPING WITH BLUSHING

PROFESSOR ROBERT J. EDELMANN is a Chartered Clinical, Forensic and Health Psychologist working in private practice. From 1986 until 1997 he was involved in Clinical Psychology training at the University of Surrey. His most recent academic appointment was to a Research Chair at the University of Surrey, Roehampton, where he currently holds an Honorary Chair. Professor Edelmann is a Fellow of the British Psychological Society and a registered Cognitive Behavioural Therapist with the United Kingdom Council of Psychotherapists. He is the author of *The Psychology of Embarrassment* as well as many articles and book chapters on embarrassment and blushing. Professor Edelmann lives with his wife and three daughters in Putney, London.

Overcoming Common Problems Series

Selected titles
A full list of titles is available from Sheldon Press,
1 Marylebone Road, London NW1 4DU, and on our website at
www.sheldonpress.co.uk

Overcoming Common Problems Series

Overcoming Common Problems Series

Overcoming Common Problems

Coping with Blushing

Professor Robert J. Edelmann

First published in Great Britain in 1990 by
Sheldon Press
1 Marylebone Road
London NW1 4DU

New edition 2004

British Library Cataloguing-in-Publication Data

A catalogue record for this book is available from the British Library

ISBN 0–85969–919–6

1 3 5 7 9 10 8 6 4 2

Typeset by Deltatype Limited, Birkenhead, Merseyside
Printed in Great Britain by Biddles Ltd
www.biddles.co.uk

To Mary Bernadette
Genevieve Rebecca
Seraphina Oriana
and
Zenoushka Leanora

Contents

Acknowledgements

The first edition of this book would probably not have appeared had Kay Kershaw not originally suggested the idea and had it then not been supported by the editorial team at Sheldon Press. My wife, Mary Bernadette, read through the manuscript for the first edition and provided many insightful comments, and without her continued support the second edition would not have been possible.

The Blushing Propensity Scale on pages 35–6 is copyright © 1991 and reprinted by permission of the American Psychological Association and the author Mark R. Leary from *Journal of Personality and Social Psychology*, 1991, 60(2), p. 256.

The Self-Consciousness Scale on pages 37–8 is copyright © 1975 and reprinted by permission of the American Psychological Association and the author Alan Fenigstein from the *Journal of Consulting and Clinical Psychology*, 1975, 43(4), p. 525.

The Cognitive Somatic Anxiety Questionnaire on pages 47–8 is copyright © 1978 and reprinted by permission of Lippincott Williams & Wilkins and the author Gary E. Schwartz from *Psychosomatic Medicine*, 1978, 40, p. 325.

Preface to the Second Edition

When the first edition of *Coping with Blushing* was published in 1990 the available research literature was extremely limited. Since then a great deal of research has been published and our understanding of fear of blushing has increased accordingly. In a book chapter I wrote in 2001 reviewing the available literature in relation to blushing (see Further reading section), two-thirds of the 95 references cited had been published since 1990. Various studies have now been published examining the bodily or physiological processes thought to underlie blushing, although the exact mechanism involved is still poorly understood. New material has been included in Chapter 2 in relation to this. A number of studies have also been published in the last decade examining individual differences in 'blushing propensity' – that is, the extent to which people report that they blush in everyday situations. Reported tendency to blush has been shown to be related to fear of blushing. However, the most interesting finding to emerge from this research is that there does not seem to be a perfect relationship between reported tendency to blush and fear of blushing with actual measured changes in skin temperature. Blushing as a problem is not necessarily to do with purely external signs that are visible to others but seems rather more related to our internal thoughts and evaluations. New material has been included in Chapters 2 and 3 in relation to this. Of particular importance in this regard is the question of the appropriateness of surgery as a cure for blushing (endoscopic transthoracic sympathectomy). If, as the research evidence suggests, problems relate to anxiety about blushing rather than visible blushing *per se* then surgical intervention may well be inappropriate. This is discussed further in a new section in Chapter 2.

Finally, when I wrote the first edition of this book in 1990, there were virtually no published studies evaluating the effectiveness of psychological therapy designed to help people overcome a fear of blushing. Those that have been published in the past decade all point to the benefits of such treatment. Perhaps one of the most important findings of such studies is that during the first few weeks of therapy improvements tend to be negligible. However, as treatment continues so improvement steadily increases. It seems that, although those being treated recognized psychological factors as important in relation to their difficulties, most in fact hoped for a 'cure' that would mean they would never blush again. It was only later in therapy, as they began to think in terms of accepting and coping rather than cure, that distress decreased and improvements occurred.

As sufferers will be all too aware, fear of blushing can lead to severe restrictions to one's life. Fear of blushing is a very common and distressing problem. It is thus gratifying that the research community is beginning to answer some of the key questions relating to both our understanding and treatment of this distressing difficulty. While great strides have been made in the last decade many gaps in our knowledge remain; we hope even more of these gaps can be filled in the next decade.

Introduction

Everyone blushes and we can all no doubt recollect an embarrassing event or experience that has caused us discomfort. For some people, however, the very thought of blushing can totally disrupt their lives. This may be because they think they blush more readily, are more sensitive to the possibility that they might blush or are more sensitive to the views of others. Whatever the initial reasons, blushing in its extreme or chronic form stops being a natural reaction and becomes a reaction to be feared, a reaction that causes many people untold discomfort. The extent of this distress is evident in the many letters sent to me by sufferers, often prompted by some reference in the press to my research interest. The first article, which appeared over 20 years ago, dealt mainly with my work on embarrassment. I received a few letters asking if help could be offered for chronic blushing. As a result I produced a brief fact-sheet, 'Blushing: What it is and what to do about it'. Then, more articles appeared in the press and the trickle of letters began to turn into a flood. One article alone produced over 600 letters and I have since received thousands.

The First Edition of this book, published in 1990, was as a direct result of the letters I had received. I have since offered psychological treatment to many people who suffer from a chronic fear of blushing. Many of these have developed full-blown social phobia. That is, a marked and persistent fear of social situations; a fear of behaving in a manner that is embarrassing or humiliating. Indeed, it is now widely recognized that for an important sub-group of social phobics a fear of bodily reactions such as sweating, muscle tremors and most importantly blushing is the main cause of their social fear. Unfortunately, social phobia and fear of blushing remain an under-reported problem within society. Most fear that their problem will not be taken seriously by the medical profession, so they continue to feel isolated and alone.

Indeed, a common theme in the letters I have received is one of relief. Relief that someone took their problem seriously, relief that they were not alone, and relief that there were strategies for overcoming their difficulties. The following three comments are typical:

1

It was with great interest and enormous relief that I read your recent article on blushing. Perhaps consolation is a more appropriate word than relief. Consoled that other people do, seriously, consider blushing a real problem, and relieved that I am not totally alone in feeling this. *Mrs C, 31, Leeds*

I have suffered from severe blushing for years and had given up hope of ever being 'normal' again. I thus read with great interest your article on blushing. It was such a relief to know that there are ways to help yourself overcome this. *Miss G, 22, clerical assistant, Huddersfield*

While reading an article on the subject of blushing I felt enormous relief. For years now I have felt burdened by my blushing problem. Feeling very desperate, I very recently visited my doctor for help and advice but didn't feel as though I was being taken seriously. *Mr B, 35, teacher, Cheshire*

These comments illustrate the emotional dilemma faced by chronic blushers – blushing after all is a common reaction, as common as laughter or tears. Everyone blushes and yet this very reaction can cause some people untold misery. How can such people seek help for a reaction that seems to cause others little discomfort at all? Will they be taken seriously? Because of these fears many people will suffer their chronic blushing in silence for years, afraid to tell anyone of their distressing problem and the devastating effect it is having on their lives.

Despite the magnitude of the problem, it is only within the last ten years that fear of blushing has been referred to with any frequency in psychology books. Prior to that the only occasional reference was to erythrophobia (from the Greek words *eruthros* meaning to be red and *phobos* meaning fear). This book explores the nature of chronic blushing, explaining why it can cause some people such distress and outlining methods for coping with the problem. Where possible I let sufferers tell their own story by drawing upon the many letters I have received and comments from people I have seen in my clinic. Chapters 1–3 examine the links between embarrassment and blushing, and explain the thought processes that give rise to chronic fear of blushing and the bodily reactions associated with it. Understanding the nature of the problem can take you half-way to defeating it.

Chapters 4–9 explain what you can do for yourself to cope with chronic blushing. While explanations can be given and strategies and techniques explained, *you* are the only one who can put them into practice. This inevitably takes a great deal of work; but persevere as you can get there in the end. With practice you can use the coping strategies described in this book to control your fear of blushing. However, do not expect to stop blushing, after all, everyone blushes; the aim is to reduce your fear of and concern about blushing. Remember also that social embarrassment is not entirely negative. Imagine a person who was never embarrassed – we would no doubt think of them as brash and insensitive. A little sensitivity to one's own reactions, and empathy and sensitivity towards others can be a positive characteristic; it is too much sensitivity that needs to be controlled.

1
Embarrassment and blushing

Imagine the following situations:

- You trip and fall getting on to a bus spilling your shopping everywhere.
- You are a guest at a dinner party and spill a glass of wine when reaching for some salt.
- You arrive at a party in fancy dress and realize that everyone else is dressed conventionally.

All these situations have one common feature – they are potentially embarrassing. The associated feeling is likely to be one of extreme discomfort and a desire to escape. You may well shake, laugh nervously, stammer an apology and avoid looking at those around you; you may even blush. Embarrassment is a common experience with which everyone is familiar.

These feelings and reactions associated with embarrassment are not dissimilar to those experienced by people with a chronic fear of blushing. There are, however, a number of differences between everyday embarrassment and a chronic fear of blushing: the cause of the feeling, the intensity of the feeling, the length of time it lasts and the person's ability to cope with it. The common experience of embarrassment is created by a clearly defined event – a social accident or *faux pas*, as in the examples given above. A chronic fear of blushing may well be experienced in the absence of such an event. Looking at the similarities and differences between the sequences of events that give rise to both embarrassment and a chronic fear of blushing will give a clearer understanding of the nature of the latter problem. The coping strategies dealt with later in this book are designed to specifically break into the sequence of experiences that give rise to distress associated with a chronic fear of blushing. Understanding the reaction is a necessary prerequisite to coping with it.

Embarrassment

It is not uncommon to hear descriptions of social mishaps such as: 'It was such an embarrassing thing *to do*', '*I looked* so embarrassed', or '*I felt* so embarrassed'. This implies that there are three ways of describing embarrassment: on the basis of the social mishap itself; because of our facial expression; or because of the feeling that occurs. Figure 1 indicates the possible sequence of events.

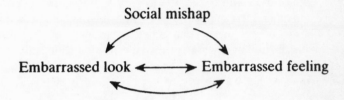

Figure 1. The vicious circle of embarrassment

In all cases of social embarrassment the social mishap occurs first in the sequence of events, causing both the look and feeling of embarrassment. Because events occur so rapidly, it is almost impossible to decide whether the look then precedes the feeling or vice versa. It is clear, however, that the look of embarrassment can make the feeling worse. Being told that you are blushing or that you look embarrassed immediately makes you feel more embarrassed; feeling more embarrassed you then look more embarrassed. A vicious circle of looking and feeling embarrassed then occurs. How can we explain these events?

Social mishaps

Our everyday meetings and conversations tend to follow a clearly recognizable pattern. For example, depending how well we know someone we may greet them either with a verbal 'Hello' or by touching, shaking hands, hugging or kissing; we will then vary the degree of personal information in the topic of conversation perhaps talking about the weather, holidays, friends or relatives; and we will then part with either a wave, a last glance or a smile. All societies and groups have unwritten rules that regulate behaviour. There are certain etiquettes and conventions that we learn as we develop within

5

a particular society or group. Even though rules are not necessarily written we know what they are and we recognize when they have been broken. Within any particular society or group the majority of people want to behave in a way that is expected by that society or group.

Linked closely with this is our general wish to create a desirable (or at least not an undesirable) impression. We don't want others to regard us as socially incompetent or physically inept. Embarrassment then has to do with our failure to present a desirable image of ourselves to others. It is generally expected that we should be able to board a bus without falling on our face; that we should be able to eat a meal without spilling anything or read a party invitation and arrive appropriately dressed. Failure to behave appropriately in a specific situation means that we are presenting a view of ourselves to the outside world that is at odds with the view we would have wished to present. And embarrassment is often the result. It is quite clear, though, that some people deliberately break social rules without feeling even the slightest twinge of embarrassment. The key word here is *deliberate* – most feelings of embarrassment result from unintentional rule-breaking.

It is also clear that there are many aspects of the particular situation and of our own psychological make-up or personality that can increase feelings of embarrassment. Spilling a drink during a coffee break with a colleague at work is likely to be less embarrassing than spilling a drink at a formal meal with the same and higher-grade colleagues. At the heart of the matter lies the fact that we value the views, impressions, opinions and reactions of others. We hope that our friends at work will understand our momentary lapse; will those who don't know us and for whom we ought to create a favourable impression think that this is what we are always like?

Situations that are novel or unusual can also affect the degree of embarrassment experienced. In any new situation where we are unsure what to say or what to do there is an increased risk of saying or doing the wrong thing and hence an increased risk of embarrassment. Although this can be a problem throughout life, adolescence, in particular, is a time when the novelty of many aspects of life can mean that it is a time of prime embarrassment. This point is dealt with in Chapter 3.

Finally, as part of our personality we differ in the extent to which we are concerned with the evaluations and reactions of others. It is obviously socially appropriate to have a certain amount of concern about the way we are evaluated; this shows empathy and regard for others. It seems clear though that being over concerned produces unnecessary worry, can lead to anxiety and hesitancy and a greater likelihood that embarrassment will be experienced. Again, this is a theme addressed in Chapter 3.

Committing a *faux pas*, or being involved in a social accident, is thus a clearly explicable starting point for embarrassment. This may result in the readily identifiable look of embarrassment.

The look of embarrassment

We are clearly able to recognize embarrassment in others from their body movements and associated reactions. When embarrassed we look away, fidget, stammer, possibly smiling or laughing and perhaps blushing. Each of these reactions has a clearly identifiable function.

Psychological research has clearly shown that the more nervous or anxious we are the more we are likely to fidget and stammer. Anxiety leads to bodily changes that are under the control of our nervous system. One result of nervous system activity is an increase in muscle tension which leads to trembling, shaking or fidgeting (see Chapter 2 for a full description of nervous system activity). Anxiety may also make us pay rather too much attention to what we are saying; the result of this is stammering.

The act of looking away, turning away or covering our eyes is clearly linked with a desire to escape. A common wish when embarrassed is that the floor will open up so that we can disappear through it. Generally speaking, however, we cannot escape from the situation but have to stay and deal with it. Although we may not be able to increase our physical distance from others we can increase our psychological distance, and one way of achieving this is by looking or turning away.

An embarrassed smile is clearly recognizable although the smile itself does not appear to differ greatly from a smile of amusement. It seems that our body and eye movements give the game away. When embarrassed we look away and start to fidget as we begin to smile; this pattern of behaviour does not occur when we are amused. Not only do we smile when embarrassed, we may also laugh, and this may serve to reduce tension and also help to create a more

7

favourable impression of ourselves. Making light of the situation may not only alleviate our own anxiety it can also help to put other people at ease.

The last but perhaps most important component of the look of embarrassment is blushing. Blushing has been described as the hallmark of embarrassment. We clearly assume that someone who is red faced is also embarrassed, although this is not necessarily the case. It is also possible to make someone feel embarrassed or to increase feelings of embarrassment simply by informing the person that they are blushing, even if they are not in fact blushing! The physiological explanation of blushing is dealt with in Chapter 2, the psychological processes that relate blushing to embarrassment are dealt with below.

The feeling of embarrassment

As indicated in Figure 1 the feeling of embarrassment is influenced by both the social mishap and the look of embarrassment. First, we turn to events around us and use our past knowledge and experience to make sense of the event that has occurred. We know when an event is embarrassing and the impact it might have on ourselves or the individual concerned. Second, we look for changes in our bodily state (heart rate, skin temperature, muscle tension, etc.) and behaviours (trembling, stammering, etc.) For example, we may notice that our heart rate has increased, that we are trembling or sweating or we may sense that we are blushing.

It seems that we only have a relatively limited amount of attention to direct towards everyday events or behaviours and that this attention can be directed either outwards to the event or inwards to our bodily state and behaviours. Thus, as our attention inward to ourselves increases, so our attention outward to others in our environment decreases.

If we have committed a *faux pas* we may direct our attention initially towards that event, perhaps labelling it as embarrassing. Our attention may then be guided specifically to those aspects of ourselves that we associate with the experience of embarrassment (fidgeting, stammering and blushing). Noticing your reaction may increase your own feelings of embarrassment so that you are caught in the vicious circle of embarrassment depicted in Figure 1. The feeling of embarrassment is then created directly by the way you evaluate both the initial embarrassing event and your own reaction to it. It is this process of evaluation that holds the key both to the experience of embarrassment and that associated with chronic fear of blushing.

It is clear that the more attention you pay to your own reactions the more intensely you experience them. Conversely, if you are able to distract yourself from your feelings you will experience them less. This notion of distraction as a method of decreasing emotional feelings provides the basis of the method for dealing with chronic blushing described in Chapter 6. It is also clear that there are a number of factors that make it more or less likely that you will pay particular attention to your own bodily reaction. These include personality factors (it seems that some people are more prone by nature to attend to their own reactions), bodily sensitivity (it seems that some people show a greater reaction than others in the same situation), and aspects of the situation itself (the larger, higher status audiences referred to earlier seem to make us more aware of our reactions).

Embarrassment, then, is an experience that results from a series of events. The starting point is a clearly defined social accident or transgression which leads to us behaving in a way that is at odds with the way we would have wished to behave. A clearly defined display consisting of fidgeting, stammering, looking away, smiling, laughing and blushing may result. The extent to which we will then personally experience any emotion of embarrassment is a direct result of our evaluation of the social accident and our reaction to it. Blushing is clearly bound up in this reaction, but how does chronic blushing differ? It is to this aspect that we now turn.

Chronic blushing

The major difference between chronic blushing and embarrassment concerns the trigger for the emotional experience. In the case of chronic blushing it is quite clear that the experience of embarrassment can be created in the absence of any clearly defined social accident, social transgression or *faux pas*. The only feature that seems to be essential is the presence of other people. The following are three descriptions given by chronic blushers of situations that cause blushing. The first is from a 22-year-old woman who commented:

9

I'm scared to talk to people because I know I will blush. I blush at home sometimes, but my family know about it and don't say anything. At work I don't get up to fetch my work in case I blush; I tell someone else to fetch it. Sometimes, just sometimes, I am all right, but most of the time I blush for no apparent reason. *Miss M, secretary, London*

The second is from a 32-year-old woman:

Any situation where I meet people really. I blush if I meet someone I know in the street. I avoid doing things that I would really love to do, such as meeting friends and relations. When they come to see me I worry all the time in case I blush. *Mrs F, Scotland*

The third is from a 47-year-old man:

Any situation that involves being with people. I hate going to places where there are a lot of people because I know I will blush. I even dread going to the doctor, dentist or seeing my children's teacher at school or even meeting old friends or relations who I have not seen for a while because I know I will blush. *Mr T, accountant, London*

Chronic blushing and the distress occasioned by it seem to occur in the absence of any clearly defined social transgression. The starting point is in fact the blush itself, or more accurately, the fear of blushing. This fear is triggered by exposure to any situation involving other people. Fear of blushing creates the feeling of embarrassment which in turn creates further blushing or fear of blushing, a pattern indicated in Figure 2.

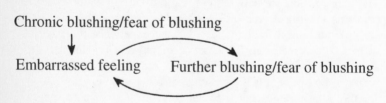

Figure 2. The vicious cycle of chronic blushing/fear of blushing

10

The vicious cycle of chronic blushing/fear of blushing

Just as you can create your own feelings of embarrassment following a social accident, so you can create your own feelings of embarrassment as a direct result of blushing or fear of blushing. This vicious cycle is illustrated in Figure 2. The series of cyclical thoughts takes the form: I am blushing (or I think I am blushing), others must see me blushing and must also think I am embarrassed, therefore I feel embarrassed, I am blushing more (or I think I am blushing more) and so on.

Comments from chronic blushers again clearly illustrate this vicious cycle. One 30-year-old woman commented:

> When I blush I think of what other people must be thinking. Things like 'She has gone bright red', or 'She is blushing', or 'She must be really embarrassed', or even 'Why is she blushing?' *Mrs S, nurse, Humberside*

A 21-year-old woman makes a similar comment:

> I wish I was one of those people whose only sign of embarrassment was a faint tinge on their cheeks. For me it is a vicious circle when I blush. I feel that my face is already pink when I meet someone, and in wondering if they're thinking about why I'm pink I go pinker. *Miss V, secretary, Middlesex*

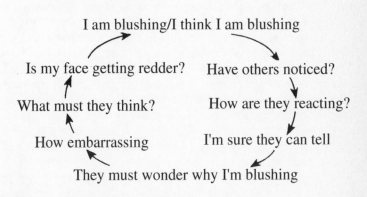

Figure 3. The blushing–thought cycle

11

It is quite clear that chronic blushers are thinking themselves into a state of embarrassment. The blush or thought that we are blushing serves as the initial trigger resulting in further thoughts about the negative consequences of blushing and a feeling of embarrassment. The pattern of thoughts is illustrated in Figure 3.

But do chronic blushers differ in some way from non-sufferers?

It is clear that the pattern of thoughts illustrated in Figure 3 could occur to anyone at some time in his or her life. By definition, however, this pattern of thoughts must occur far more frequently for chronic blushers. This raises the question of whether there are crucial differences between chronic blushers and non-sufferers. There are four possible ways in which chronic blushers might differ.

First, chronic blushers by nature might be more physiologically sensitive; they might require less exertion or stress to produce heart rate or body temperature changes. Second, their blushes might be more visible: perhaps chronic blushers genuinely redden more than non-sufferers. (The physiological possibilities are not discussed here but are dealt with in Chapter 2; coping strategies linked to this are dealt with in Chapter 5.) Third, by nature, they may be more prone to concentrate on their own thoughts and bodily reactions. Fourth, and related to this, they may tend to catastrophize about both the possibility of blushing as well as their actual blushes; in other words fear of the prospect of blushing may be as central as fear of blushing itself.

In other words, although chronic blushers may blush more readily and their blushes may be more visible it is not necessarily this possibility that is central in creating feelings of embarrassment. A crucial aspect seems to be that chronic blushers are more sensitized to their own bodily reactions, more likely to attend to them and more fearful of the possibility that they may blush. As we have already seen, in making judgements about embarrassment we may attend either to an outside event or to ourselves. If you are more sensitized to your own reactions you will naturally direct your attention towards your own real or imagined bodily reaction. The reaction you may think is clearly visible to an observer may not be visible at all – you are the only one who knows you feel embarrassed!

The likelihood that we will attend to aspects of ourselves rather than to events around us is a part of our make-up, our personality. The tendency to reflect about ourselves is termed self-consciousness and, by nature, some people seem to be more self-conscious than others. Research suggests that there are two aspects of self-consciousness: an awareness of our unseen thoughts and feelings (private self-consciousness) and an awareness of our observable actions and behaviours (public self-consciousness). People who are privately self-conscious are more likely to reflect about themselves a lot and to generally be aware of and attend to their inner feelings. Someone who is publicly self-conscious is more likely to be concerned with what other people think of them, worrying more about making a good impression in comparison to someone who is not publicly self-conscious.

Psychological studies have shown that people who are shy, socially anxious or easily embarrassed are likely to be publicly self-conscious. Worrying about what other people think is clearly a part of chronic blushing. Chronic blushing for some may therefore relate to shyness or anxiety about social situations.

The picture is rather more complex than this, however. Although some chronic blushers worry about others' reactions a crucial element in chronic blushing is a tendency to over concentrate on one's own reactions; that is, a tendency to be privately self-conscious. Psychological studies have shown that private self-consciousness is much less likely to be related to shyness, social anxiety or being easily embarrassed. My own research, however, shows that some chronic blushers are privately self-conscious. Chronic blushing in this case is unrelated to shyness or anxiety about social situations but is linked to a clear over concentration on one's own thoughts and feelings. (You will be able to assess your own level of private and public self-consciousness by completing the series of questions presented in Chapter 3.)

There is clearly not just one explanation for chronic blushing: some chronic blushers may be shy; some may over concentrate on private thoughts and feelings; some may be physiologically sensitive; for some, reddening may be more visible. Any person's reason for chronic blushing may be derived from one or more explanations.

The following comments illustrate the many possible explanations for chronic blushing.

At present I blush as a symptom of being a shy/emotional person and it is preventing me or I am letting it prevent me from living a normal life. *Miss W, shop assistant, Belfast*

It's bad enough knowing you're blushing, but when people decide to tell you you're blushing it's unbearable. I find it so difficult to stop myself thinking about my blushes – many times I have felt so conscious of myself that I have had to make excuses to leave the room. *Mrs H, 43, teacher, Birmingham*

I seem to blush very easily, especially in hot rooms. I notice myself becoming hot and this makes me feel embarrassed although I'm not usually embarrassed and not shy. *Mr P, 30, bank employee, Manchester*

While certain facets of chronic blushing may differ from person to person, in all instances a central underlying concern relates to a fear of blushing and the imagined negative consequences of this. It is this fear that activates the typical chain of thoughts illustrated in Figure 3. However, just as there are differing facets of chronic blushing, so there is more than one coping strategy. These strategies are linked to particular facets of blushing so that certain strategies or combinations of strategies may be more appropriate than others for some people. In each instance a central focus is to reduce the fear of blushing and not to eliminate blushing *per se*. Chapter 4 deals specifically with strategies for selecting appropriate coping techniques. But first, we will examine the physiological reaction we call blushing and its individual differences in more detail.

2
What is blushing?

This chapter explains why we blush and looks at individual variations in the visibility of blushes and in sensitivity to blushing. Explanations of the bodily or physiological processes giving rise to chronic blushing can be translated into explanations of methods for coping. If we know what mechanisms give rise to blushing then we should be able to identify ways for reversing the blushing process. As the following comments illustrate, blushing tends to be located in specific areas of the body most notably the cheeks, forehead and ears, but also the neck and upper chest. Blushing can also be associated with other symptoms such as sweating, a pounding heart, a sinking feeling in the stomach, trembling hands and a general panicky feeling.

Every time I meet people I have a blushing attack. I feel my face going red which makes my heart beat faster and my face gets even hotter. Not only does my face go red but my neck and forehead as well – a very bright red. My face stays this colour and I begin to panic and invariably I end up not doing whatever I was going to do. *Mr A, 40, Tyneside*

One blushing incident that occurred more than ten years ago still haunts me. I was working in a bar and one day two girls I knew walked in – they were coming over to the bar and I could feel my face turning very red. The feeling became very panicky and I felt that everyone must be wondering what was wrong with me. I couldn't think of words to say, my legs felt weak and my hands sweaty. I could think of nothing other than my red face. *Mr B, 30, computer operator, London*

My blushes seem to come from my stomach. Someone will speak and my stomach jumps, my heart races and my face and neck redden. I feel hot and flustered and cannot make my words come out in the way I want them to. The red blotches seem to remain on my neck for ages afterwards. *Mrs P, 39, housewife, Wigan*

As such, blushing is part of an emotional reaction triggered by exposure to any situation involving other people. One result of this reaction is for our body temperature to rise; facial reddening is part of the mechanism associated with the cooling of our body so that it can maintain a relatively constant temperature. In order to explain blushing it is therefore necessary to explain first the bodily or physiological reaction associated with emotions, and second the way the temperature of our body is controlled.

Emotional reactions

Bodily changes associated with emotional states are under the control of our nervous system. We can think of our nervous system as the communication network of our bodies with the brain as the headquarters, a 'computer' centre where all the major decisions are made. It is a very complex structure composed of a number of interconnecting parts. Set at the very base of the brain is a small area of nervous tissue called the hypothalamus. This is closely connected to the pituitary gland, the 'master gland' within our bodies. The relative position of these two parts of the brain is shown in Figure 4. The hypothalamus has a number of crucial functions, two of which are related to emotional control and blushing:

- It ensures our body temperature is kept normal because it is sensitive to blood temperatures above or below normal. The hypothalamus appears to contain control mechanisms that detect changes in various aspects of our bodily functioning (including bodily temperature); it then operates to correct the imbalance.
- It acts as the 'go-between' for emotional events almost as if it is linking the mind and the body in its actions. The hypothalamus will act on signals (such as the identification of an event as 'embarrassing') sent from higher centres of the brain (the cerebral cortex – see Figure 4), relaying further signals to the pituitary gland which will then secrete appropriate hormones. One hormone, secreted under conditions of stress, acts on a further gland (the adrenal gland, located just above the kidneys) which in turn releases a chemical called adrenaline which causes nervous perspiration, makes the heart beat faster and so on.

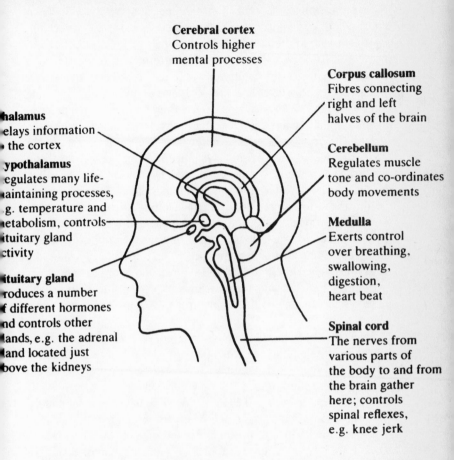

Cerebral cortex
Controls higher
mental processes

Corpus callosum
Fibres connecting
right and left
halves of the brain

Cerebellum
Regulates muscle
tone and co-ordinates
body movements

Medulla
Exerts control
over breathing,
swallowing,
digestion,
heart beat

Spinal cord
The nerves from
various parts of
the body to and from
the brain gather
here; controls
spinal reflexes,
e.g. knee jerk

Thalamus
Relays information
to the cortex

Hypothalamus
Regulates many life-
maintaining processes,
e.g. temperature and
metabolism, controls
pituitary gland
activity

Pituitary gland
Produces a number
of different hormones
and controls other
glands, e.g. the adrenal
gland located just
above the kidneys

Figure 4. The human brain showing the relative positions of the
hypothalamus and pituitary gland

Apart from the nervous system located in the brain (the central nervous system), we have a complex system of nerves running down either side of our spinal cord (peripheral nervous system) which are controlled and co-ordinated by the hypothalamus. These peripheral nerves consist of two divisions with a pair of nerves (one from each division) linking to various organs within the body (heart, lungs, eye, digestive organs, etc.). The mass of nerves that come from the middle part of our spinal cord is referred to as the sympathetic division. Impulses through these nerve fibres are transmitted by the secretion of a chemical called adrenaline. Nerve fibres that begin from above and below this system form the parasympathetic division. The chemical transmitter used by this division is called acetylcholine. The two divisions of the peripheral nervous system are illustrated in Figure 5. The chemicals they secrete tend to have opposite reactions on the body, the sympathetic division having a similar effect to the adrenal gland under conditions of stress. Thus, the sympathetic system speeds up heart rate, while the parasympathetic slows it down; the sympathetic increases the rate of breathing, the parasympathetic slows it down; the sympathetic increases the dilation of the pupils in the eyes, the parasympathetic decreases it.

When we experience an intense emotion, such as embarrassment, fear or anger, we are aware of the bodily changes that result from the activation of the sympathetic nerves: heart rate increases, breathing becomes more rapid, mouth becomes dry and so on. Our nervous system is preparing our bodies for action. You have no doubt noticed that when animals are frightened or otherwise alarmed the hair on their backs and tails will bristle and stand on end. This is similarly activated by the sympathetic nerves and the 'gooseflesh' we experience is the comparable reaction in human beings. In fact these emotional reactions are reflexes by our bodies to an emergency situation and have been referred to as the *fight* or *flight* response. We are being prepared for defence by being filled with 'energy'. Unfortunately, however, because blushing is associated with a social context, rarely will either fight or flight be appropriate. We are forced by social constraints to remain in the situation, thus not allowing the emotion to dissipate. It is only when the emotion subsides that the parasympathetic system takes over, conserving our energy and returning us to our normal state. Activation and

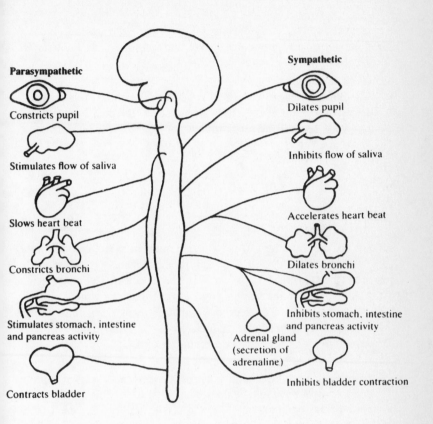

Figure 5. The peripheral nervous system showing the sympathetic and parasympathetic divisions

maintenance of sympathetic nervous system activity is thus associated with blushing.

My heart beats very fast and I feel my pulse racing. I can't breathe properly, my voice shakes and I blush profusely. *Miss M, 16, Hertfordshire*

The pulse in my neck starts to pound, my breathing feels panicky; I feel shaky and eventually start sweating. By this time my face has gone red and my eyes start watering. *Miss C, 23, journalist, Hertfordshire*

The skin and blood flow

One further action of the sympathetic nervous system is to close or constrict the blood vessels in the skin while increasing the flow of blood to the muscles. This is again part of the fight or flight mechanism as blood is shifted from regions where it is not urgently needed (the skin) to those where it is (the muscles). The constriction of blood vessels in the skin is why we sometimes go white with fear. Why then should we go red with embarrassment if blushing is part of an emotional response associated with sympathetic nervous system activity? There are two main reasons:

- Although the sympathetic nervous system can act as a unit in conditions of psychological stress, it is also possible for different parts of the sympathetic system to act separately from each other or even in opposite directions. Blushing is an example of such an action; the blood vessels in the facial region are prevented from constricting while other sympathetic activity (caused by sympathetic nerves activating sweat glands) takes place. A similar response occurs in warm environments when sweating (caused by sympathetic nerves activating sweat glands) with facial flushing which results from the inhibition of sympathetic nervous system activity.
- Not all areas of the skin have the same patterns of circulation. The blood vessels in the face, neck and upper body can open or dilate at the same time that blood vessels in other parts of the body, such as the feet and hands, can close or constrict.

Part of the reason for these complex reactions is that our skin, together with our hypothalamus in the brain, plays a vital role in the regulation of our body temperature. The hot, flustered feeling associated with blushing is a direct result of the physical response to emotional arousal described above. Our facial reddening is then simply a sign that our body is overheating and attempting to cool down.

Blood supply and temperature regulation

Our skin is a two-layered complex of cells and connecting tissues. Running throughout the inner layer is the skin's rich blood supply contained within capillaries. These blood vessels, spreading out rather like the branches of a tree, are referred to as the cutaneous vascular system. It is the opening and closing of these blood vessels that help to regulate our body temperature. The opening of the blood vessels, referred to as vasodilation, means that a larger volume of blood is nearer the surface of the skin allowing blood heat to be lost. Because this involves dilation of the cutaneous blood vessels the technical term for blushing is peripheral cutaneous vasodilation! A term that would no doubt carry far fewer negative connotations than blushing!

Anything that creates an increase in body temperature, whether exercise, a hot room or emotional arousal associated with anxiety about what people think of us, will result in some vasodilation to prevent our body from overheating. This is then visible as a flushed face.

My blushing seems to get worse in a warm atmosphere, or when I do physical activity – my face ends up looking like a beetroot. *Mr C, 35, unemployed, Newcastle*

A typical situation when I blush is when I have been outside in the cold for quite a while and then enter a warm building. In fact going into a hot room always seems to make me blush; only slightly if I am alone; if the room is full of people the blush is considerably worse. *Miss K, 24, secretary, Wolverhampton*

Whenever I meet new people I blush, particularly if the room is

21

hot. Blushing affects my life by restricting activities I would like to take part in – I avoid pubs and clubs because the rooms tend to be hot – I blush whenever it gets hot in a room. For example, blushing seems to increase when I have been in a warm office for a while. *Mr H, 27, shipping clerk, Manchester*

The opposite will happen in a cold environment when our blood vessels constrict, referred to as vasoconstriction. When this happens a smaller volume of blood is nearer the surface of the skin so our body is able to retain heat. Our faces will then be much paler in complexion as described above. Blushes thus disappear if we both literally and metaphorically 'keep cool'.

Once, in order to stop my blushes, I used a spray to freeze my neck. It actually worked for a while but my blushes came back when the effect of the spray wore off. *Mrs F, 50, Ayrshire*

I always have a glass of iced water with my meal or sit near an open window. This seems to keep my blushes down. *Mr H, 20, Worcestershire*

In overall control of the regulation of our body temperature is the hypothalamus. When our body overheats this registers in the hypothalamus which causes nerve impulses to be sent to the skin. This results in increased sweating and vasodilation which cools our body down. Sweat glands that are specifically associated with temperature regulation are more concentrated in the palms of our hands and the soles of our feet and to a lesser extent in the forehead. These are brought into action not only by changes in environmental temperature but also by emotional reactions. Our skin is cooled down as heat is extracted from it by evaporating sweat. The face, hands and feet are thus the most important areas for regulating body temperature. Blushing is a sign that our body is doing its job – it is cooling us down.

Variations in blood supply and skin thickness

Cutaneous blood vessels are not evenly distributed within the skin. In fact, regularity seems to be the exception rather than the rule. The irregularity is responsible for the blotchiness associated with blushing experienced by some people.

When I blush my whole neck and chest seems to become very red. While my face blushes my neck always seems to be red and blotchy making me feel very uncomfortable. I now wear clothes that cover my neck and chest. *Mrs J, 37, accounts clerk, Lancashire*

There are marked differences in skin thickness in different parts of the body as can easily be seen if we compare the skin on our eyelids with the skin on the soles of our feet. If the skin is particularly liable to wear and tear (for example if we do a lot of manual work with our hands) it can become even thicker in response to the demands put upon it. In addition, there are marked individual differences in skin thickness. The sayings about being thin skinned and sensitive or thick skinned and insensitive can be taken quite literally in this context. We differ in the extent to which our blushes are visible.

I am a fair-skinned woman with thin facial skin. When I blush I start to go red on my cheeks and ears, but worse than that I go all red and blotchy on my chest and upper neck. *Mrs H, 35, teacher, Sussex*

Being blond and blue-eyed with fair skin my problem with blushing is severe as it shows considerably even if I am only slightly embarrassed. *Mrs T, 36, secretary, Merseyside*

As many aspects of our make-up are inherited it would not be surprising if skin characteristics and, hence, our propensity to blush is also inherited. Although the existence of a family pattern to blushing might be taken as evidence for an inherited blushing trait, it could simply mean that we are more likely to learn our actions and reactions from those nearest to us. No doubt both learning and inheritance play some part in the family pattern to blushing noted by many people.

Blushing is not only a problem for me; my mother also blushes very easily, as does my brother, albeit to a lesser extent. *Mr D, 21, law student, Buckingham*

My father was anxious and highly strung and I have my father's nature. He had the same problem, suffering very badly from blushing. *Mrs P, 36, Wigan*

23

Blushing seems to be a family problem: both my mother and my younger sister suffer as well. *Miss W, 23, teacher, London*

Blushing and fear of blushing

So far in this chapter the bodily mechanism underlying blushing has been examined. It is evident from this that facial reddening is a normal everyday experience with which everyone is familiar. Facial reddening varies both with regard to the situations that provoke it (for example exercise versus social exposure) as well as across individuals (thin versus thick skinned). It is only facial reddening in social contexts that is referred to as blushing and it is generally only such instances of facial reddening that occasion distress. However, it is interesting to observe that while many people who blush report great distress at their experience many others do not.

A number of research studies have shown that actual blushing, that is measurable increases in skin temperature, is *not necessarily* related to reported intensity or frequency of blushing. In the last ten years a number of studies from various countries (USA, New Zealand, UK and the Netherlands) have found no relationship between actual blushing and self-reported frequency of blushing. In most of these studies participants were allocated to groups according to the extent to which they either reported blushing (their blushing propensity – see Chapter 3 where you will have the opportunity to complete the Blushing Propensity Scale) or were afraid of blushing. They then took part in a social task during which their facial skin temperature was continuously measured. The two groups were then compared on actual blushing and reported intensity of blushing. A consistent finding across all studies was that there were no differences between the groups with regard to the actual skin temperature changes. However, those who were afraid of blushing or who reported blushing more frequently *thought* that they blushed far more intensely than those who were not afraid of blushing. Why is this finding important? Well, clearly and perhaps surprisingly, when you think your face is bright red this may not actually be the case. Indeed, when you feel you are as red as a beetroot you may well be the only person who perceives this to be the case. Many people with a pink tinge to their cheeks do not think of themselves as chronic blushers as they do not have a marked concern about the possibility

24

that they might blush. The crucial aspect of chronic blushing is *not necessarily* actual blushing but the underlying psychological parameter, fear or anxiety about blushing. This clearly has important implications for both physically and psychologically based treatments.

Can drugs help?

After a great deal of thought I went to my GP and explained my blushing problem. She gave me some tranquillizers to take twice a day although they do not seem to be having much effect. *Mrs C, 40, Lancashire*

As we shall see in Chapter 4, even if drugs were able to dampen down the symptoms in order to see us through in the short term, they do not provide us with strategies that put us in control and hence able to cope with the situation in the long term. But do drugs have any effect on blushing? Sympathetic nervous system activity can certainly be reduced by taking sedatives. As this would keep bodily arousal under some degree of control it could also decrease both actual blushing as well as anxiety about blushing. However, few people have reported that drugs have helped to control their blushing in the longer term and research suggests that drug treatment for chronic blushing/fear of blushing may only be of limited value.

Can surgery help?

I am a chronic blusher and have been since a teacher humiliated me in school when I was 16. I am 22 now and was so depressed with the worsening situation that I paid for the operation to try to stop the blushing. That was about four weeks ago now, and although I am trying to keep positive, realistically I don't think the operation has worked for me. *Miss P, 22, Hull*

In recent years a number of newspaper and magazine articles have appeared claiming dramatic success for surgery as a 'cure' for chronic blushing. The procedure, referred to as endoscopic transthoracic sympathectomy, involves interrupting the sympathetic nerve pathway to the face, thus effectively destroying the neural circuitry that controls blushing to emotional events. Surgery will then reduce facial reddening in someone prone to blush excessively.

The attraction of such a treatment is obvious – it promises an 'instant cure' – very different from the hard work involved in engaging in psychological therapy and the lengthy process of learning to cope more effectively. However, while there is increasing evidence for the effectiveness of psychological therapy and in particular cognitive-behaviour therapy, as a treatment for chronic blushing, there is little by way of long-term evaluation of the success of surgical intervention. Information suggests that patients report satisfaction with surgery when asked about its effectiveness shortly after having undergone the procedure. However, a number of side effects have also been reported, including compensatory sweating – that is, inappropriate bodily or facial sweating and flushing, particularly while eating. Such symptoms are likely to be as distressing as the fear of blushing, hence patients opting for surgery may be no better off in the long term.

A central question with regard to any treatment is whether it is appropriate. There is little evidence to indicate that those who are likely to pursue surgical treatment for blushing actually blush more readily or intensely than other people. As noted above, the central problem often relates to fear or anxiety about blushing rather than actual blushing *per se*. If the central problem is indeed one of anxiety or fear then anxiety would be the more appropriate target for treatment rather then surgical intervention to permanently eliminate the normal regulation of facial blood flow. One reason why people report that surgical intervention has reduced their blushing may be because they think they are blushing less and hence are less anxious about the prospect of doing so.

Sensitivity to chemical additives

As well as individual differences in skin thickness we also show variations in skin sensitivity. Sensitive skin can show an exaggerated reaction to chemical additives in soaps or make-up, increasing the likelihood of a red face and hence increasing concern with blushing. It is also possible that sensitivity to certain additives in food increases the likelihood of being red faced.

I have found that niacin affects my blushing greatly. I am not shy and not worried about doing something embarrassing – it is my

26

red face that makes me feel embarrassed. I have eased my problem considerably by avoiding bread and flour products that contain niacin. *Mr H, 20, Wolverhampton*

Nicotinic acid or niacin occurs naturally in many food including yeast, beans and lean meat. Our body requires it for converting food into energy. Niacin, produced commercially by the oxidation of nicotine with nitric acid, is thus added to many food products. In his book *E for Additives*, Maurice Hanssen notes that nicotinic acid can dilate blood vessels and, if taken in large amounts, can produce facial flushing. He also notes that many other additives including calcium sulphite and hexamine, which are used as preservatives, can cause skin sensitivity or irritation.

If you have particularly sensitive skin or if you think you react to certain foods try avoiding those products or foods that you think are responsible for your red-faced appearance. You should be able to work this out by a process of trial and error. Only in relatively few cases though will this form of sensitivity be responsible for increased blushing. However, even when such a physical explanation can be found it still provides only part of the answer. This form of reaction may clearly cause physical discomfort or distress; the distress only becomes emotional when we become concerned about the way other people regard the reaction; that is, in much the same way that blushing without such a physical cause becomes distressing.

Sensitivity to bodily changes

Not only are there individual differences in the visibility and distribution of our blushes, there are also marked variations in the extent to which we are aware of our bodily reactions. Some people are sensitive to very minor fluctuations in skin temperature which would pass unnoticed by others. Our expectations about our own reactions do not match those of the people watching us. Also, some people can clearly identify the situations that provoke their blushes – they are 'cued in' to those situations: blushing is anticipated. Clearly these differences in reactivity and sensitivity have important implications both in terms of creating concern about blushing and when learning to cope with blushing. As blushing is associated with

27

bodily arousal, then learning to control this arousal will in turn lead to a diminution of blushing. Relaxation training, as outlined in Chapter 5, deals specifically with this. As we also differ in our sensitivity and expectations about blushing and the reactions of others, altering these expectations and the attention we pay to others' reactions will also decrease our anxiety about and general concern with blushing. Anything that distracts our attention away from our own bodily reactions will serve to ease the problem. The process of redirecting thoughts outlined in Chapter 6 deals specifically with this. Before turning our attention to the selection of appropriate coping strategies we will examine in rather more detail the psychological factors that determine who blushes or rather those factors influencing individual differences in concern about blushing.

3
Who suffers?

This chapter examines reasons for age-related differences in the impact of blushing and also explains why we are differentially affected by concerns about blushing. As you will see, a central factor related to concerns about blushing is self-consciousness. You will have the opportunity to assess both the extent to which you believe you blush in everyday situations and how self-conscious you are by answering a series of questions. You might want to complete these questions two or three times over the coming months to see whether the scores you obtain decrease as you follow the suggestions outlined in Chapter 7 for increasing self-confidence and decreasing self-concern. But is it possible to describe exactly who suffers from blushing? The following comments suggest that a typical sufferer will be a shy, self-conscious adolescent.

I have suffered from blushing since I was 16 and it has got worse over the years. I am now 37 with a teenage son, yet the situation has taken over my life. *Mrs M, teacher, County Kildare*

When I was young and going through my teens I suffered very badly from blushing and the very thought that something or somebody might make me blush stopped me doing things I wish I had done. *Miss F, 29, writer, Leeds*

Blushing has affected my life for as long as I can remember – you see I have always been shy, nervous and self-conscious. This has made it very difficult for me to join in with social activities leading to the additional problem of loneliness. *Miss J, 24, shop assistant, London*

My problem started when I was at school. I could never speak in class in case I blushed. I never had any confidence in myself – my blushing always got in the way. *Miss G, 25, local government officer, Birmingham*

Although there is an element of truth in the description of a typical sufferer as a shy, self-conscious adolescent, in fact the picture is far more complicated. Adolescence is certainly a period when many people suffer problems with blushing. For some, blushing will then decrease as the adolescent years are left behind; for others, the problem will remain or, as the above comments suggest, may even get worse. People who are naturally shy, inhibited or self-conscious are also more likely to suffer problems with blushing than their outgoing, sociable counterparts. Many blushers are nevertheless friendly, sociable and outgoing and no longer adolescents, yet they suffer public agonies because of the fear of blushing. This is illustrated in the following comment.

I have been a sufferer since about the age of 15, I am now 23 – I thought that the problem would decrease with age! It's strange because I do have an outgoing personality and want to do lots of things and also have many friends but as soon as I feel people's eyes on me I go a deeper shade of red very quickly. *Miss R, librarian, London*

The key feature in all cases, however, is self-consciousness. Age differences in the nature of self-consciousness explain why we suffer more severe problems with blushing at certain ages. The fact that, by nature, some people seem to be more self-conscious than others also explains why we are differentially affected by concerns about blushing. Understanding why certain people suffer more at certain ages can help us understand the general nature of blushing.

Age and blushing

At what age does blushing start?

Clearly the faces of very young babies have the capacity to redden but it is unlikely that we would call this blushing. A number of psychological studies suggest that the earliest recalled memories of blushing seem to be from the age of five. The most frequent reported ages for the emergence of blushing as a problem is, however, between the ages of nine and 13 with the problem often becoming more severe during the adolescent years. This is illustrated in the following comment.

I remember being worried about my blushes from as early as five; I was concerned about being teased and would dread being late for things in case anyone would notice or comment. The worst of my problems, though, seemed to start around the age of 11 when I would dread being asked a question at school or if attention was drawn to me by comments from family or friends. From then on my adolescence was a distressing and embarrassing time – my face would colour at the slightest things. *Mrs B, 63, business woman*

Why are there age differences in blushing?

There are several important age-related changes in our understanding of ourselves and our social environment which explain age-related changes in the way blushing affects our lives. Before the age of five we tend to see things (including ourselves) from our own point of view – we have difficulty putting ourselves in someone else's shoes. At about the age of five we begin to gain an impression of what we are like from someone else's viewpoint – how we appear to others. It is clear therefore that if we are unable to see ourselves from someone else's point of view we are unlikely to be concerned about the view they have of us.

In addition, it appears that around the age of five our knowledge of right and wrong in relation to social rules also begins to change. As we grow up the rules of society are learned through reward (with affection, treats and so on) for appropriate behaviour and punishment for inappropriate behaviour. One of the most widely used forms of punishment is laughter, teasing and ridicule – literally punishment by humiliation and embarrassment. Younger children will realize, because of the laughter, they have behaved inappropriately without necessarily knowing the meaning of their behaviour. The coyness typical of younger children may be a reflection of this. At about the age of five we begin to realize not only that we have behaved inappropriately but also why our actions appear to be wrong. In other words we know why our behaviour is likely to prompt laughter, teasing and ridicule – in short that our behaviour is embarrassing.

These age-related changes mark a crucial stage in the development of conscious awareness of ourselves. At about five we begin to develop an understanding of the way our blushes are labelled by other people – that inappropriate behaviour is perceived by others as

embarrassing and that blushing is perceived as a sign of embarrassment. Inappropriate behaviour, embarrassment and blushing thus
become events to avoid.

A child who is self-conscious by nature may be more upset by
teasing, laughter and blushing than his or her less self-conscious
peers. Learning experiences will also differ; some children may be
exposed to more frequent laughter, ridicule and teasing or the need
to behave 'correctly' may be over emphasized. In some cases this
may well lead to a general over concern with one's blushes in later
life.

Why is blushing a particular problem during adolescence?

During adolescence we seem to pass away from merely seeing things
from someone else's perspective to actually thinking about the
thoughts of other people. Psychologists suggest that this reflecting
about what others are thinking leads to the adolescent constructing
an 'imaginary audience'. As young children we are only concerned
about other people's view points when we can actually see the
people themselves; as adolescents we develop the capacity to
become over concerned about what other people might think, even
when those people are not actually present. We begin to fear that we
may be noticed or that we may be singled out for attention; we have
fears about what others might think of us or that we may do the
wrong thing. These fears are illustrated in the following comments.

In school, the lessons I dread most are the language lessons, for
the teachers like us to take part orally – but I don't dare to
because I know I will blush and if they ask me something, of
course I go bright red and sometimes I get really scared. Simply
sitting in class and someone smiling at me can send my cheeks
red. I get all worked up walking down the corridors to lessons in
case someone asks me a question. *Miss W, 14, Manchester*

A further aspect of adolescence is that it also marks a time of
dramatic change. Our bodies alter rapidly in size, shape and
functioning; secondary sex characteristics develop and many aspects
of life are new. As adolescents we are faced with a rapidly changing
lifestyle – we are no longer children but not yet adults. We no longer
want to behave like children but have yet to acquire the skills of an
adult. This is particularly true of opposite sex friendships when as

adolescents we are unsure where to begin – 'crushes' on unattainable adults are not unusual. The attentions of someone we like can be enough to create the brightest of blushes – what if they suspect? What if our friends know?

> One incident I shall never forget was during a biology lesson at school. I, unfortunately, fancied the biology teacher and so every time he looked at me or asked me a question I coloured up. He, seeing this, would always tease me and in front of everyone ask why I was blushing. One day when he asked 'Why are you going red?' one of my classmates said 'Because she thinks you fancy her, Sir.' I blushed so fiercely that tears welled up. *Miss R, 27, clerk, Leeds*

Conversely, we may be afraid of blushing in case we make 'that' someone think we actually do have a 'crush' on them.

> I have noticed that some people send me red, but others don't bother me; it is something about the person and this I notice with teachers. It is really embarrassing because there must be a few male teachers who think I have a crush on them. Some male teachers even when they ask me seemingly basic and trivial things will make me go bright red. *Miss W, 14, Manchester*

Another major problem can be that daunting 'first date'. An adolescent is not sure how a 'real man' or 'real woman' should act with a member of the opposite sex – they have neither the experience nor the skill. We may wish to ask someone for a date or encourage someone else to ask us but are unsure how to proceed. We are naturally anxious and inevitably become flustered and embarrassed with our blushes giving the game away. As we acquire the experience and skill many of our fears disappear or at least decrease but for many the nervousness and embarrassment may endure well past adolescence and into adulthood. It may be that for many of us adolescence is such a difficult time that we never acquire the skills or ability to cope with these situations.

> Being noticed by people makes me blush, especially with members of the opposite sex. My social life is non-existent and I have never had a boyfriend or a relationship. As soon as any

conversation is directed towards me I feel my face becoming extremely red which makes contact with people very difficult. *Miss B, 25, staff nurse, Cumbria*

I have female friends and enjoy going out with them; I get on better with my own sex because I don't feel as though they are looking at me in the same way that a man would; I don't feel threatened by them. Yet it makes me very unhappy to admit that I have never had a boyfriend; I want to lead a normal life, get married and have children yet I don't see much chance of this happening. *Miss E, 24, administrative assistant, Liverpool*

Blushing as we get older

It is generally assumed that from adolescence onwards both frequency and fear of blushing decline. Indeed, there is evidence that the neurochemical receptors that control the dilation of the facial veins become less numerous with age and hence ones' capacity to blush may well decline. It is also likely that many of us become less concerned about other people's evaluations of us as we get older. Interestingly, however, and in spite of these factors, fear of blushing for some, as noted earlier, may actually increase with age. Because we assume blushing is a problem of adolescence and hence something we will 'grow out of' we see continued blushing as we get older as a continuing sign of social awkwardness. However, our continuing concern is more likely to be related to self-consciousness and fear of blushing rather than to actual frequency of blushing *per se*.

I have been blushing for 50 years; having been an inwardly anxious but outwardly confident teenager, at 15 I experienced my first blush which I found so disturbing it has preoccupied me ever since. As I have got older my difficulties seem to have become worse rather than better. In certain social situations I tend to panic, become inwardly very upset and imagine I must look very red faced, something I thought I would grow out of – I think most of the problem is that I am far too preoccupied with my self-image – I desperately want people to think I am the capable and confident person they must expect a 65-year-old career woman to be. *Mrs S, 65, Liverpool*

Clearly then, age-related changes in our conscious awareness of ourselves relate to age differences in the impact of blushing. Many of our adult concerns may result from unpleasant learning experiences as young children or adolescents. Being excessively teased as a child or fumbling and failing as an adolescent can have a marked impact in later life. These learning experiences undoubtedly interact with aspects of our physiological make-up, as described in Chapter 2. A fair-haired, thin-skinned child or adolescent with visible blushes may have a more difficult time than his or her thicker-skinned counterpart. Being thicker-skinned may be both a physiological and metaphorical factor. Some people may be less prone to dwell on aspects of themselves such as their blushes or may be less concerned with others' views about them. Their personality may be such that they are less self-conscious by nature.

Personality and blushing

As noted throughout this book, we differ both with regard to our reported tendency to blush and our fear of blushing. Most of you reading this book are doing so because you suffer chronically with blushes and fear of blushing. A useful scale, the Blushing Propensity Scale, has been developed specifically to assess our perception of the extent to which we blush in everyday situations. This assessment is made up of the following 14 statements which may or may not describe situations in which you blush. Read each statement carefully and then choose the phrase from the rating scale that best describes the extent to which you feel you would blush in each situation described. Then place the number you choose in the box next to each question.

1 = I never feel myself blush in this situation
2 = I rarely feel myself blush in this situation
3 = I occasionally feel myself blush in this situation
4 = I often feel myself blush in this situation
5 = I always feel myself blush in this situation

1 When my teacher or boss calls on me in class or at work   □
2 When talking to someone about a personal topic   □

35

3 When I'm embarrassed ☐
4 When I'm introduced to someone I don't know ☐
5 When I've been caught doing something improper or
   shameful ☐
6 When I'm the centre of attention ☐
7 When a group of people sing 'Happy Birthday' to me ☐
8 When I'm around someone I want to impress ☐
9 When talking to a teacher or boss ☐
10 When speaking in front of a group of people ☐
11 When someone looks me right in the eye ☐
12 When someone pays me a compliment ☐
13 When I've looked stupid or incompetent in front of
   others ☐
14 When I'm talking to members of the other sex ☐

(The original questionnaire was developed with students –
question 1 has been changed from the original to include work as
well as college situations.)

Scoring and interpretation: This is very straightforward – simply
add up your total score from the boxes. The range of possible scores
with this scale is 14–70. It is unlikely that many of you reading the
book, given your fear of blushing, will score less than 60 and many
will score the maximum possible. Scores obtained by a mix of
people, regardless of whether or not blushing is a problem tend to be
in the region of 35–45. You might wish to compare the score you
obtain now with scores you obtain over the coming weeks and
months when you have been practising the strategies outlined in the
second half of this book.

The Blushing Propensity Scale has been used to examine
differences in the extent to which men and women report that they
blush as well as the relationship between blushing and other aspects
of our personality, including self-consciousness.

As mentioned in Chapter 1, research suggests that there are two
aspects of self-consciousness: an awareness of our inner thoughts
and feelings (private self-consciousness) and an awareness of our
observable actions and behaviour (public self-consciousness). Both
are related to a tendency to worry about our blushes. The more
concerned we are with both our own behaviour and the views of
others, the higher the standards we set ourselves and hence the more

likely it is that we will fail to meet those standards. The more concerned we are the more flustered we become and hence the more likely it is that we will blush or think we are blushing.

How self-conscious are you?

Take a look at the extent to which you worry about what other people think of you. The following assessment is made up of 23 statements which may or may not be characteristic of how you see yourself as a person. When you have read each one carefully choose the phrase from the rating scale, shown below, that best describes how characteristic each statement is of you. Then place the number you choose in the box next to each question (ignore the A, B and C labels until you have completed the questionnaire).

1 = extremely uncharacteristic
2 = generally uncharacteristic
3 = equally characteristic as uncharacteristic
4 = generally characteristic
5 = extremely characteristic

1 I'm always trying to understand myself. A ☐
2 I'm concerned about my style of doing things. B ☐
3 I'm very aware of myself. A ☐
4 It takes me time to overcome shyness in new situations. C ☐
5 I reflect about myself a lot. A ☐
6 I'm concerned about the way I present myself. B ☐
7 I'm often the subject of my own fantasies. A ☐
8 I have trouble working when someone is watching me. C ☐
9 I constantly scrutinize myself. A ☐
10 I get embarrassed very easily. C ☐
11 I'm self-conscious about the way I look. B ☐
12 I find it difficult to talk to strangers. C ☐
13 I'm generally attentive to my inner feelings. A ☐
14 I usually worry about making a good impression. B ☐
15 I'm constantly examining my motives. A ☐
16 I feel anxious when I speak in front of a large group. C ☐
17 Before I leave the house I always look in the mirror. B ☐
18 I sometimes have the feeling that I'm off somewhere watching myself. A ☐

19 I'm concerned about what other people think of me.   B ☐
20 I'm alert to changes in my mood.   A ☐
21 I'm usually aware of my own appearance.   B ☐
22 I'm aware of the way my mind works when I go
   through a problem.   A ☐
23 Large groups of people make me nervous.   C ☐

Scoring: Add up the scores for boxes marked A, B and C to give you three separate scores. The A score represents your degree of private self-consciousness (awareness of your unseen thoughts and feelings), the B score represents your degree of public self-consciousness (awareness of your observable behaviour and actions), the C score represents your degree of social anxiety (the extent to which concerns about yourself affect your ability to deal with everyday encounters). In looking at the interpretations given below do not worry if you have obtained a high score. Remember that some insight into your own actions and some sensitivity about what others might think are both positive qualities to possess. But, you need to bring too much sensitivity under control; the suggestions given in Chapter 7 will help you to achieve this. As mentioned at the beginning of this chapter you may wish to repeat the questions every two or three months to see how much you are beginning to get things more under your control.

Interpretation
A – Private self-consciousness
High score (above 29): You do tend to spend a great deal of time reflecting about yourself, analysing your every move. In fact, you are rather too sensitive about the way events affect you.
Medium score (23–29): Just about the right balance of insight and reflection.
Low score (below 23): You tend to avoid thinking about why you do things, in fact self-discovery is not for you.

B – Public self-consciousness
High score (above 22): You are very concerned with what others think of you. In fact, you are rather too sensitive to others' evaluations, feeling easily hurt or inadequate.
Medium score (16–22): Just the right balance of concern about what others are thinking – you are self-confident yet aware of the impressions other people form of you.

38

Low score (below 16): You have little concern about what others think; either you are very self-confident or you are not really aware of how you appear to other people.

C – Social anxiety

High score (above 16): You are very unhappy about social situations that involve a degree of evaluation by others. You are constantly thinking about what others might be thinking about you. **Medium score** (9–16): Although you might be anxious in some social settings you are generally confident about how you appear in public.
Low score (below 9): You are self-confident and have little concern about social situations.

If blushing is a concern, it is most likely that you will have obtained a high score for public self-consciousness, although you additionally may have obtained a high score for private self-consciousness. You tend to focus on your own thoughts and actions, dwelling on what others might think of you. Altering this pattern of thoughts is central to dealing with chronic blushing and is described in Chapter 6, and building self-confidence is dealt with in Chapter 7. Before leaving the question of 'Who blushes?', however, we will end this chapter by looking at whether men or women suffer more from blushing.

Gender and blushing

Although women tend to obtain higher scores than men for both public and private self-consciousness, the difference between their scores tends to be slight. This suggests that there should be little difference between men and women in the extent to which they suffer difficulties with chronic blushing. Although a few studies suggest that women report both a greater fear of blushing and greater tendency to blush in everyday social situations, for the most part research, particularly using the Blushing Propensity Scale, indicates that men and women do not differ in this regard. However, while real gender differences may be slight there may well be gender differences in the extent to which blushing is acceptable. In earlier centuries it was far more acceptable for women to blush. In Victorian England, for example, a shy, coy, blushing girl was considered attractive, and blushing in women was considered flattering. This was no doubt part of the expectation that Victorian women would play a secondary role in society, that they should be reserved and inhibited in their behaviour. As Western society has changed so has the need for women to develop the assertive skills that have traditionally been expected of men. Nevertheless many men see blushing as devastating as it is seen as a sign of weakness and hence as men they should not blush.

I blush crimson at virtually anything, anybody, and anywhere, with male or female, young or old. I am an administrator in a school for girls aged 12 to 19. Just imagine at the age of 45 and being a man how I feel. It's terrible. *Mr C, Buckingham*

I used to work as a welder, but since losing my job I have not been able to obtain another one. I blame it on my blushing. How can anyone take a 23-year-old man seriously if he goes puce if someone so much as speaks to him? *Mr A, unemployed, Tyne-and-Wear*

I sometimes feel a bit inferior because, being a man, I think it is less acceptable to have a fear of blushing. Although it may be more acceptable for a woman, a man really cannot be a shrinking violet. *Mr T, unemployed, Derbyshire*

With the changing role of women in society, blushing is now also seen by women as unacceptable. Yet for women blushing is likely to be more visible because of their thinner, less rugged skin complexions. Thus, while the social notion that men should not blush might make blushing worse for men, women's physical make-up might mean that blushes are more readily visible for a larger proportion of women. The common feature reported by both men and women is the feeling that other people will not take them seriously if they blush.

Imagine standing in a ward full of patients and blushing over something silly so that everyone can see. In fact, after a while I was well known for it and people seemed to enjoy teasing me and staring when it happened which made it worse. I love my job but because of my blushing I wonder how anyone can take me seriously. *Mrs T, 35, nurse, Yorkshire*

Other well-qualified people with responsible jobs also indicated the problems posed for them by blushing.

> I am a 53-year-old veterinary surgeon and, being successful at my job, I am often asked to give talks to veterinary colleagues. I blush from the start but this is worse if I am asked a question requiring some thought. I am left thinking they cannot possibly take anything I say seriously. *Mr D, Lancashire*

> Since qualifying as a barrister I have never appeared in court. The reason being that my blushing is so severe I feel that if I did get on my feet no-one would take me seriously. *Miss J, 31, barrister, Norwich*

Whether male or female, the vicious circle of blushing and thoughts about what we imagine others may be thinking gradually erodes our confidence. Increasing concern about blushing can create a downward spiral of despair with gradually increasing social isolation. At first social events are avoided, and then friends and colleagues, even work may be avoided until isolation is complete.

> I'm a 47-year-old man whose life has been ruined by blushing. My social life is very limited; I don't go anywhere where there are crowds and if I do have to go out with my wife I sweat and blush if we meet anyone and want to hide. I always feel as if every one is watching me and noticing my blushes. Keeping a job is almost impossible because I blush even in a simple conversation. I usually leave my job when I feel that other people working there have noticed my blushes. You suddenly realize that you have virtually cut yourself off from people because of your blushes. *Mr R, Cardiff*

In the remainder of the book we look at how to break into this vicious circle: how to reverse the pattern of negative thinking and decrease the concern with blushing. Working your way back up the spiral can be hard work and there may be slips along the way but it can be done. Start by telling yourself 'I can and I will'.

4

Coping with blushing: Some preliminary comments

Coping with embarrassment

At the beginning of Chapter 1 are three examples of embarrassing situations: tripping and falling when entering a bus, spilling a glass of wine at a dinner party and arriving at a party inappropriately dressed. All three situations consist of social accidents or *faux pas* which result in others seeing our unfortunate behaviour. We may want to escape, run away or wish that the floor would open up so we could disappear, but it is always too late, we have already been exposed. It is our own behaviour that has given rise to our embarrassment, and others who have seen it may regard it as embarrassing – regardless of whether we blush or not. Under these circumstances there are many coping strategies we could use to redress the balance and present ourselves in a more favourable light: we might apologize, attempt to excuse or justify our behaviour, or tackle the situation in a humorous way.

By apologizing we are accepting responsibility for the embarrassing event. At the same time, saying sorry allows the situation to be passed over quickly and forgotten by those present. An apology is all that is required in some situations but in other instances we may additionally need to explain our actions by excusing or justifying them. This consists of attempts to lay the blame for our actions with something or somebody else. We can seek to excuse our behaviour by claiming that it was accidental, that we did not intend to behave in the way we did, that it is just part of our nature to do such silly things, or we might even seek to blame someone else. Thus, we might blame a slippery floor for our fall, our own clumsiness for spilling wine, or our forgetfulness for not remembering that a party was fancy dress. On other occasions the appropriate use of laughter or joking can make light of the situation, transforming it from an embarrassing to a humorous event.

Embarrassment involves public exposure of our inept behaviour; coping attempts tend to involve drawing further attention to ourselves. But whereas embarrassment involves negative attention, our coping strategies involve attempts to make the attention favourable rather than unfavourable. We are endeavouring to show people that our embarrassing behaviour is unusual and not typical of the way we normally behave. Our coping strategies are endeavours to show that we are normally skilled, adept and competent people.

Coping with blushing

Coping with blushing presents a wholly different dilemma: one of the central concerns for chronic blushers is how to *avoid* drawing attention to themselves. When blushing, or feeling that we are blushing, the major wish is to hope that no-one has noticed; the last thing we want to do is draw further attention to ourselves by apologizing, excusing or joking about the way we imagine we must look. Sometimes we are forced to comment if someone else comments about our appearance, but generally our major concern will be to escape, hide or diminish our blushes. In fact, many blushers will try to avoid or leave the situation in which they blush.

I know exactly what makes me blush and live in dread of those occasions. It does not matter who I am with – family, friends or complete strangers – I usually end up making some stupid excuse and rush off somewhere. *Mrs M, 24, shop assistant, Hampshire*

I constantly feel as if everyone is watching me and seeing my blushes. It often becomes too much to bear so I end up either making an excuse to leave the room, or just walk outside or hide somewhere until I have cooled down. *Mrs D, 18, Wales*

I fear people talking to me because I know I will blush; it is on my mind all the time. As soon as someone starts talking to me I want to stop talking as soon as possible so that I can get away as quickly as I can. *Mrs W, 30, Bangor*

The fear that our own appearance will let us down and, if it does, our inability to pass comment about it, explain why coping with blushing can present such severe difficulties. In fact, for many people the only way to cope is to use methods that they feel will hide their possible blushes. Many women wear make-up or high-necked clothes as the following comments illustrate.

I have probably exhausted all the ways to hide my blushing. I have used green foundation make-up to tone down the colour of my skin. I wear high-necked clothes, pull my hair forward and avoid situations where I feel uneasy – I can sense those situations as though I have some kind of built-in radar. *Mrs W, 44, estate agent, Bristol*

I like to have a sun-tanned face as it helps the blushes merge with my complexion. Artificial powders and blushers help and glasses cover up some of my face. *Mrs F, 50, sales assistant, Cambridge*

I have solved the problem by wearing thick foundation cream, with a green cream underneath. I put this face on when I get up and take it off last thing at night. I still blush but I don't look bright red. *Mrs M, 41, Humberside*

Many men resort to alcohol in an attempt to boost confidence and decrease concern about blushing, even though alcohol may create an even redder face or additional problems.

I rarely leave the house except to go to the pub and even then I have to have several drinks first. That is the only time I can talk to people and forget about blushing. Unfortunately as a result drink has also become a problem; some of my friends have never met me when I am sober. *Mr T, 31, Derby*

As mentioned in Chapter 2, both men and women have resorted to tranquillizers in an attempt to feel less anxious about their red faces.

Eventually things became so bad that I plucked up the courage to tell my GP about my problem. He prescribed Valium which seems to prevent me from becoming so worried about my blushes but the problem is still there and seems to be getting worse again. I don't want to keep taking tablets; I just want to be able to cope with my blushes. *Mrs N, 31, secretary, Reading*

I have thought about leaving my job because of my blushing. In the end in order to keep my job I went to my GP who prescribed tranquillizers. I take five tablets a day to try to ease the problem, but I still feel that I can't cope when I am at work. *Mr N, 45, geologist, Edinburgh*

44

All the above strategies involve physical remedies: sufferers hope either that the problem can be hidden from view or that a tablet will make the problem disappear. As noted in Chapter 2, some even resort to surgery in the hope that their problem can be eliminated by physical means. Unfortunately, these are not really remedies at all: they may help people face some situations and just occasionally may help people to think differently about themselves but usually the problem is still there and still has to be coped with.

> Before I go to work in the morning I put lots of brown make-up on my face – it's the only way I can get out. I know that my blushes will then be less visible. Even so, I frequently blush for no apparent reason, even if just having a conversation with someone. I know that I am blushing. This makes me get flustered and upset, although because of the make-up I get by. *Mrs M, teacher of handicapped children, County Kildare*

Simply covering up what we believe to be the problem does not make it go away and does not provide us with control over our difficulties. The only remedy is to learn strategies that enable us to cope; strategies that put us in charge of the situation. This does not mean that blushing will ever go away – we all blush and it is a fact of life – but it is possible to decrease concern about the situation by using various distraction techniques and to reduce the reddening itself by use of calming and relaxation strategies. Many blushers have tried these strategies, although for some this is with seemingly limited success.

> Please do not suggest relaxation as it does not seem to work. I try to relax when I feel a blush coming on but it still spreads up my neck and across my face. *Mrs N, 32, administrator, Reading*

Others report that the techniques only work some of the time.

> I have attempted to remedy the situation by relaxing myself, breathing deeply and slowly, and concentrating on the people around me. On occasions this does seem to resolve the problem although at other times I still 'crack'. *Mr H, 21, student, Stoke-on-Trent*

Others persist and work hard to overcome their problems.

> Over the past few months my blushing is happening less. I began to practise relaxation and to give myself positive suggestions. Then I realized that when I knew I was going to blush, something like this would always go through my mind: 'Oh no, it's going to happen – what can I do to get away from this situation/ conversation, I'm so stupid.' I'd be sweating and panicking and blushing like mad. So I made myself try to change my thoughts to something like, 'Yes, I'm probably going to blush, I'll just carry on this conversation, look people in the face and feel calm and cool.' After a while I realized the blushes weren't so bright red and I began not to worry quite as much. I still blush but it's getting less and I feel more in control. *Mrs T, 35, nurse, Yorkshire*

The important point is to learn the appropriate strategy or combination of strategies and to apply them effectively by practising and persisting in your efforts to master the problem. Practising and persisting are really the key words and will be emphasized throughout the latter part if this book. In the remainder of this chapter we examine how you can identify appropriate strategies or combinations of strategies. The systematic manner in which you must learn and practise them will be outlined in the second half of the book.

Blushing: thoughts and bodily reactions

In the first three chapters discussion has centred on the fact that blushing consists not only of a bodily reaction but also of thoughts about blushing. The blushing-thought cycle is illustrated in Figure 3 in Chapter 1. In Chapters 2 and 3, evidence suggesting that there is not necessarily a one-to-one relationship between actual blushing and fear of blushing has also been referred to. In other words, our coping attempts should be aimed at reducing our concern about blushing, regardless of whether this concern is related to actual or perceived facial reddening. However, such concerns can be reduced both by making us feel we are really blushing less as well as by altering our beliefs about and interpretation of our perception that we are blushing. In other words coping strategies can and should be

46

directed both towards our actual bodily reaction as well as towards the thoughts involved. As such, we tend to differ in the extent to which we concentrate on either our bodily reactions or our thoughts. These differences can be used to determine the starting point for your coping attempts.

If you are more prone to concentrate on your bodily reactions, then the calming and relaxation strategies described in Chapter 5 provide a useful starting point. If you are more prone to concentrate on your own thoughts then it is more useful to start with the distracting techniques described in Chapter 6. Although the starting point may differ, the eventual aim is to combine different strategies effectively so that you are able to feel more in control of the situation. By gradually controlling your bodily reaction and your thoughts about such reactions so your confidence will grow. However, there are a number of additional steps you can take to enhance your self-confidence so that you are more positive about yourself and the assumed reactions of others. These are described in Chapter 7.

Do you concentrate more on your thoughts or your bodily reactions?

The following scale will help you to find out the relative importance of your thoughts and your bodily reactions in determining the distress caused by blushing. It is made up of 14 statements that may or may not reflect how you react in typical blush-inducing situations. Read each statement carefully and then choose the phrase from the rating scale shown below that describes best the degree to which you generally or typically experience that particular symptom when in a blush-inducing situation. Then place the number you choose in the box next to each question (ignore the letters A and B until you have completed all the questions).

1 = do not experience at all
2 = experience very slightly
3 = experience somewhat
4 = experience quite a lot
5 = experience very much

1 I find it difficult to concentrate because of
   uncontrollable thoughts.   A ☐

2 My heart beats faster.   B ☐

3 I worry too much over things that do not matter.   A ☐

4 I feel jittery in my body.   B ☐

5 I imagine terrifying scenes.   A ☐

6 I get diarrhoea   B ☐

7 I can't keep anxiety-provoking pictures out of my
mind.   A ☐

8 I feel tense in my stomach.   B ☐

9 Some unimportant thought runs through my mind
and bothers me.   A ☐

10 I pace about nervously.   B ☐

11 I feel like I am losing out on things because I can't
make up my mind soon enough.   A ☐

12 I become immobilized.   B ☐

13 I can't keep anxiety provoking thoughts out of my
mind.   A ☐

14 I perspire.   B ☐

Scoring: Obtain two separate scores by adding up the seven scores next to each box marked A and the seven scores next to each box marked B. Your A score is your thought score and your B score your bodily reaction score, both having a possible range of scores of 7–35. In looking at the interpretations given below do not worry if you have obtained a high score – there are occasions when everyone has worrying thoughts or bodily reactions associated with anxiety. The important thing is to recognize how you react so that you can select the appropriate strategy to help you control your reaction rather than being in a position where your reaction controls you. Practising the strategies described in the next three chapters will enable you to gain the necessary coping skills.

Interpretation:
A – Thought score
High score (above 22): With this score you are someone who has a lot of distressing thoughts that disrupt your ability to concentrate. You tend to worry a great deal about your blushes.
Medium score (15–21): Although you have some worrying thoughts about blushing there are many situations in which you probably cope quite well.
Low score (less than 14): You do not really spend too much time or

energy mulling over distressing thoughts. Thinking about blushing is not really a problem for you.

B – Bodily reaction score

High score (above 22): With this score you are certainly very aware of your bodily reaction and may well be a person (described in Chapter 2) who notices even minor fluctuations in bodily state. You will certainly be very aware whenever you start to sweat, if your heart pounds, if you have cold or clammy hands, a dry mouth, or stomach distress, and you will most certainly be aware of your blushes.

Medium score (15–21): Although you may well notice your bodily reaction you may be able to cope by calming yourself down in some situations.

Low score (below 14): You are only mildly aware of your bodily reaction and blushes may actually go unnoticed.

Clearly it is possible to obtain different scores for bodily reactions and thoughts as indicated in Table 1.

Table 1. Possible combinations of thought score and bodily reaction score

	Bodily reaction score		
Thought score	Low	Medium	High
High	A	B	C
Medium	D	E	F
Low	G	H	I

Thus, A represents a low bodily reaction score but a high thought score, B a medium bodily reaction score but a high thought score, C high scores for both bodily reactions and thoughts and so on. Which letter represents you? If you have a higher bodily reaction than thought score (that is F, H or I) you will find it most useful to turn to Chapter 5 and learn how to deal with bodily reactions by using calming and relaxation strategies before dealing with distracting techniques described in Chapter 6. If you have a higher thought than bodily reaction score (A, B and D) you will find it most useful to turn to Chapter 6 and learn how to deal with distressing thoughts by using distracting techniques before dealing with relaxation strategies described in Chapter 5. If you are in the C category (high bodily reaction and thought score) then both techniques will prove to be equally useful and you will need to incorporate aspects of both in dealing with your difficulty. The same applies, but to a lesser extent, to those in the E category (medium bodily reaction and medium thought score), although your difficulties are likely to be less pronounced. You are unlikely to fall into category G (low bodily reaction and low thought score) as this would imply that you are neither very aware of your bodily reaction nor do you experience distressing thoughts – unlikely for someone who suffers from blushing.

How to cope

A package of strategies for coping with blushing will be presented in the next three chapters. These involve learning to calm yourself down, redirecting thoughts and redeveloping self-confidence. Each technique will be described and a series of exercises presented. A summary of critical points in the programme is also presented in Chapter 8. Emphasized throughout is the need to practise – and keep on practising – the techniques in order to get to a position where you are able to control your own reactions. This does not mean that you will never blush again, but it does mean that, with practice, you will be able to stay calm, and thus blush less; keep your thoughts away from blushing, and thus prevent yourself from increasing your blushing; and present yourself in a more confident and less self-conscious manner. It can be done as the following comment illustrates. This was sent to me by Mrs W, a 37-year-old sales representative from West Yorkshire after receiving a copy of my fact-sheet:

Thank you for sending me your fact-sheet which I found to be of great help. I would like to say that having practised your suggested ways to reduce blushing, to my astonishment they have actually worked! In the knowledge that I am starting to control my blushing behaviour, my confidence is slowly but surely returning. In fact, I felt confident enough to tackle an 'assertion course' through my company. I found this a tremendous help, adding to the skills I had already developed as a result of your fact-sheet. It has been a long, slow struggle but it is certainly worth all the hard work. I feel like a totally new person.

5

Calming yourself down

Fear of blushing and awareness of changes in skin colour or body temperature clearly lead to increased tension and anxiety and further facial reddening. The vicious circle described earlier of blushing, thoughts about blushing and further blushing is established with increased physical arousal and physical sensations. One way of breaking into this cycle is to learn to decrease the physical arousal, tension and anxiety experienced, with the result that less facial reddening will occur. This can be achieved by learning to stay calm and relaxed even in those situations that provoke the most anxiety. This chapter describes relaxation exercises and the techniques you can use in order to learn how to relax.

Learning to relax is like any other skill: it takes a great deal of practice. Very often we fail to recognize how tense we are until it is too late. With regular practice we are more aware of the tension so can quickly do something about it. Knowing how to relax not only allows you to be generally calmer, it also helps you to calm down in situations that make the blushes begin. As long as you know how to relax you can remind yourself to stay calm and relaxed. Reactions like those described below will then become a thing of the past.

> In any social situation I find that my level of anxiety increases and the blushing starts. I don't seem to be able to free myself of this tension and talk coolly, I just seem to blush more and more. *Mrs M, 54, occupational therapist, London*

> Public occasions are purgatory. I just feel so tense and nervous knowing that as soon as I stand up in front of parents I will go scarlet. Staff meetings are impossible – how can I look responsible when I just become very red? The tension is so bad that it is giving me high blood pressure. *Mrs H, 52, head teacher, Lincolnshire*

What is relaxation?

Training in muscle relaxation involves systematically tensing and relaxing the muscle groups of the whole body. Together with breathing exercises and practice, it is possible to learn to become relaxed quite quickly. After all, it is impossible to feel tense and relaxed at the same time. Practice is the key word and you should try to go through the exercises for about 20 minutes, twice a day. An ideal way to practise is in a comfortable position with your eyes closed. If this is not possible twice a day then you can make do with any situation, even for five minutes while sitting at your desk in the office or in your car while stuck in a traffic jam. But remember, only regular practice will enable you to receive the maximum benefits. Let's start, though, by identifying the major muscle groups and one way to tense each. The way of tensing described is not the only way and may not be the best way for you – you may use alternatives if you wish.

The muscle groups

1 and 2 *Right and left hand*: These can be tensed by clenching your fist with the palm faced down. In doing the exercises you should start with your dominant hand followed by the non-dominant.

3 and 4 *Right and left arm*: These can be tensed by holding your arms straight by your side and pushing your arms inwards towards your body. Again you should start with your dominant arm and follow this with your non-dominant.

5 and 6 *Right and left foot*: These can be tensed by pushing your foot away from you, curling your toes downwards as you do so. Again you should start with your dominant side and follow this with the non-dominant.

7 and 8 *Right and left leg*: These can be tensed by extending your leg so that it is straight and pushing downwards as if against some imaginary object. Alternatively, you can lift your leg in front of you still pushing outwards and away from your body. Again you should start with your dominant side and follow this with your non-dominant.

9 *Stomach*: This can be tensed by pulling in your stomach as much as you can.

10 *Shoulders*: These can be tensed by pushing your shoulder blades backwards and upwards as if you were trying to make them touch.

11 *Back of neck*: This can be tensed by pushing your chin downwards towards your chest. Prevent your chin from actually touching your chest by pretending that an imaginary object is in the way.

12 *Forehead*: This can be tensed by raising your eyebrows and wrinkling your forehead.

13 *Eyes and lower forehead*: These can be tensed by pulling your eyebrows down and closing your eyes tightly.

14 *Lips*: These can be tensed by pressing your lips together tightly.

Preparing for the exercises

Start by finding somewhere quiet, warm and comfortable – an armchair is ideal or you may find it preferable to lie on your bed. It is better not to do your relaxation practice when you are in a hurry or after a big meal. Make sure you are not wearing any restrictive clothing, such as shoes, and take off your glasses or remove contact lenses if you wear them. You may find it more relaxing if you turn off the lights and you should keep your eyes closed whenever you practise the exercises. Make sure that you are as comfortable as possible before beginning – you might find it useful just to sit still for half a minute in order to get settled.

The tension–relaxation cycle

When you are comfortable the next step is to alternately tense and relax each of the muscle groups identified above. A way of achieving this is described below. For each muscle group there are five key elements to remember:

1 Tense each muscle group for 5–10 seconds but for no longer. You should not break your concentration by timing yourself. A rough idea of timing can be achieved by repeating the word 'tense' to yourself slowly 4–5 times or by counting up to 15.
2 When tensing attend to the sensations of tension in that particular muscle group and part of your body.
3 After 5–10 seconds say the word 'relax' to yourself, releasing the tension as you do so. Let the tension go suddenly, allowing your whole body to go loose and heavy.
4 For each muscle group tensed and then relaxed make sure that you notice the difference between the tensed and relaxed state.

54

5 Between tensing each muscle group allow yourself about 20–30 seconds to relax completely. Again, you should not break your concentration by timing yourself. A rough idea of the time can be achieved by slowly repeating the following instructions to yourself: 'I am going to let myself relax ... I am going to unwind ... I am going to let the feeling of relaxation pass over me ... as I relax I am going to take a deep breath [*breathe inwards deeply and slowly*] relaxing as I breathe out [*breathe out slowly*].' You can repeat this to yourself each time if you wish or compare the sensations of each of the muscle groups you have tensed and relaxed. There is no magic wording to use and you can change the wording to suit yourself. You could simply repeat the word 'relax' to yourself while breathing deeply and imagining the tension draining away from your muscles.

Learning to relax

You should repeat the tension–relaxation cycle for each of the 14 muscle groups listed above. You should start with your dominant hand, followed by your non-dominant hand, then your dominant arm followed by your non-dominant arm and so on. You may find that each cycle lasts about 60 seconds so that the full set of exercises for all 14 muscles will last almost 15 minutes. The following are sample instructions for the tension–relaxation cycle for the first two muscle groups:

I am going to start by tensing the muscles of my right hand – tense ... tense ... tense ... tense ... and ... relax. As I relax I am going to note the difference between the feeling in my right hand now and the feeling I had when it was tensed a few moments ago. I am now going to let myself relax ... I am going to unwind ... I am going to let the feeling of relaxation pass over me [*breathe inwards deeply and slowly*] relaxing as I breathe out [*breathe out slowly*].

Now I am going to pass on to the muscles in my left hand – tense ... tense ... tense ... tense ... tense ... and ... relax. As I relax I am going to note the difference between the feeling in my left hand now and the feeling I had a few moments ago. I am now going to let myself relax ... I am going to unwind ... I am going to let the feeling of relaxation pass over me [*breathe inwards deeply and slowly*] relaxing as I breathe out [*breathe out slowly*]. I am going to compare the relaxed feeling in my left hand with the relaxed feeling in my right hand.

To begin with you might find it easier to practise just one or two muscle groups until you are sure what to do. Once you are familiar with both the procedure and the muscle groups to work on you should be able to go through the whole process without having to refer back to the book.

Deepening exercises

After completing the tension–relaxation cycle for each of the 14 muscle groups you should allow yourself several more minutes to deepen your feeling of relaxation. This can be achieved in three phases by self-talk and attention to breathing.

1 You might begin by repeating the following to yourself as you count very slowly from one to five:

As I count I am going to become more and more relaxed ... further and further down into a deep restful state of complete relaxation ... [*ONE*] ... I am becoming more restful and more deeply relaxed ... [*TWO*] ... I am getting deeper and deeper into a relaxed state ... [*THREE*] ... [*FOUR*] ... more and more relaxed ... [*FIVE*] ... completely relaxed.

2 You should then attend to your breathing, repeating the following to yourself three or four times:

I am going to remain in a very relaxed state while concentrating upon my breathing. I am going to breathe in slowly and deeply through my nose feeling the cool air as I breathe in [*breathe in deeply and slowly holding your breath in for 2–3 seconds*]. I am now going to breathe out slowly through my nose feeling the warm air as I breathe out.

3 You should complete the exercises by combining self-talk while breathing deeply, repeating the following five phrases to yourself:

i   I am going to let myself become more and more relaxed, letting my muscles go loose ... heavy ... and ... relaxed.

56

ii As my muscles become relaxed I am going to sink deep into the chair, my muscles becoming more and more comfortable.

iii My breathing is regular and deep . . . with each breath I take my relaxation becomes deeper.

iv I am feeling warm, heavy and completely relaxed.

v A very deep state of relaxation is moving over all the areas of my body.

Alternative deepening exercises

An alternative to telling yourself to relax as you breathe is to make use of calming images. You will find this particularly useful if you are good at picturing peaceful and soothing scenes – a sandy beach or a grassy bank beside a stream, for example. Imagine you can hear peaceful sounds, such as birds singing, or the waves on the seashore and that you can touch the soft grass and feel the warmth of the sun. The scene can be imaginary or it can be somewhere you know – just as long as you can lose yourself in its sight, sound, smell and feel. You should be able to feel warm and comfortable, alone and at peace. The following is an example you might try:

> Imagine you are above a beach looking down at a beautiful bay. The sun is shining from a cloudless sky. There are stairs leading down to the bay and you begin to walk down the steps. With each step you become more and more relaxed [*you can count the steps if you wish using each number to let your body feel warmer, heavier and more relaxed*]. It is a beautiful hot day, and you can feel the warmth of the sun on your body. You can see the golden sand getting nearer and can see and hear the waves as they gently splash on to the beach. Keep counting down the steps allowing yourself to become more relaxed as you count. Eventually, you reach the beach and stretch out on the sand feeling its warmth against your body. Continue to watch and listen to each wave as it gently laps against the sand. Slowly count the waves, allowing yourself to become more and more relaxed as you count.

Allow yourself to stay with your relaxing image as long as you like. Use the same image each time you practise your relaxation exercises. Eventually, even under very distressing blush-inducing circumstances, you will be able to use your calming image as a place to retreat to in your mind. Remember, though, that learning to relax and to make use of relaxation strategies takes practice.

Ending the exercises

The entire relaxation cycle, and breathing and deepening exercises, will have taken you at least 20 minutes. Do not try to jolt yourself out of your relaxed state but let yourself return to an alert state gradually. You might count backwards from five to one allowing yourself to move a little more with each number. Thus, as you say five you might move your hands and arms; on four move your legs and feet; on three move your body; on two your head and on one open your eyes allowing yourself to return to your normal alert state while remaining calm and relaxed.

Practising and record keeping

In order to receive the maximum benefit from relaxation practice is essential. It will take some time before you are able to gain the maximum benefit from relaxation but persevere. Remember, blushing has presented you with difficulties over a long period of time – it was not a problem that emerged overnight. Therefore, you should not expect to reverse the process overnight. Gradually, you will improve your ability to relax quickly as an active way of coping when you begin to blush. If you find it particularly difficult to practise from the instructions in this chapter then cassettes with relaxation instructions are available commercially from many retail outlets.

In order to help yourself to practise you will find it useful to keep a daily diary using a format such as that in Figure 6. Make up a series of sheets so that you can use one each week. Make a note after each practice session of any thoughts or feelings you have and any muscle group you find particularly difficult to tense and relax. These may well require more effort in your subsequent practice sessions. Also rate your level of tension both before and after each session using the following seven-point rating scale:

1 = completely relaxed throughout my body
2 = generally relaxed through most of my body
3 = slightly more relaxed than usual
4 = neither relaxed nor tense
5 = slightly tense in some areas of my body
6 = very tense in some areas of my body
7 = extremely tense throughout my body

You can then not only make sure that you have kept to your daily practice schedule but also look back to assess any changes in feelings of tension and relaxation as a result of practising the exercises.

Figure 6. Record of daily relaxation practice

Week number _____

Date _____

Day		Tension rating (1–7)	Comments about general feelings during practice and any difficult items
Monday	Practice 1	Before	After
	Practice 2	Before	After
Tuesday	Practice 1	Before	After
	Practice 2	Before	After
Wednesday	Practice 1	Before	After
	Practice 2	Before	After
Thursday	Practice 1	Before	After
	Practice 2	Before	After
Friday	Practice 1	Before	After
	Practice 2	Before	After
Saturday	Practice 1	Before	After
	Practice 2	Before	After
Sunday	Practice 1	Before	After
	Practice 2	Before	After

Making relaxation work

After two or three weeks of regular, daily practice you should find that you are able to calm yourself when you put your mind to it. You should also be more aware of the particular way that specific situations affect you. Now is the time to really put the relaxation strategies into action. By trial and error you will be able to find out which components of the exercise programme help you in which situations. You might find that simply by saying the word 'relax' to yourself and taking a few deep breaths you are able to stop a blush in its tracks. When in a blush-inducing situation you may find that your rate of breathing quickens and your heart rate increases. Concentrate on your breathing until it is deep and even – you will soon feel less flustered. By understanding what happens to your body you can use parts of the relaxation exercise programme to good effect.

Remember also that you do not need to wait until you are blushing and flustered before you attempt to calm yourself down. If you know you are going to be in a social situation where blushes have been inevitable in the past, prepare yourself by making sure that you are as calm as possible before the event. Blushes that were sudden and uncontrollable before will then happen less often. When they do happen remember that you can still cope by saying 'relax' to yourself or by concentrating on breathing evenly. It may take a few seconds but it will work. With hard work and practice you will find that learning to relax helps you to cope with blushes.

I have worked hard at trying to relax. At first it was difficult to stay calm when I knew I was starting to blush but I now feel as if I am beginning to win the battle. I also keep myself calmer generally which helps as well. Knowing that I can cope also makes me feel more confident and I am doing things now that I wouldn't have dreamt of doing six months ago. *Mrs N, 38, teacher, London*

6

Re-evaluating and redirecting thoughts

The way our pattern of thinking creates a fear of blushing and further facial reddening is described in Chapter 1 and illustrated in Figure 3. By first recognizing and second understanding the pattern of thinking associated with fear of blushing it is possible to cope by re-evaluating your beliefs and redirecting your thoughts away from what you imagine others might be thinking. In this chapter, methods of assessing, monitoring and changing patterns of thinking are presented. As with learning to relax, understanding and re-evaluating your pattern of thinking requires a great deal of hard work and practice. At first you may find it difficult to break a well-established pattern of thinking but with regular practice you will gradually be able to substitute this with new, more positive and helpful thoughts. This may take time but do not be discouraged if you feel you are not being immediately successful – persevere – change, when it happens, will be extremely rewarding. The first step in promoting change is to recognize and identify the important aspects of your way of thinking that promote blushes. Remember from previous chapters that there is not necessarily a one-to-one relationship between actual visible blushing and fear of blushing. It is often the fear that we might be blushing and the negative thinking pattern associated with this that occasions so much distress, when our actual blushes may not even be noticed by those around us.

Negative thinking

Just as some blushes seem to happen suddenly so some thoughts about blushing seem to pop in to our minds even when we are not thinking about blushing. They occur rapidly and automatically and generally consist of negative thoughts about ourselves and our reaction.

I blush at the slightest thing, such as someone approaching and talking to me: I feel the blush instantly and it's a case of 'Oh no, not again'. *Mr B, 42, cashier, Lancashire*

At other times we worry about blushing before it happens and tend to think very negatively about the impression we will create.

> When someone talks to me it's an ordeal because I know I'll blush. *Mrs F, 26, technician, Wigan*

> I am afraid to speak in case I make a complete fool of myself by blushing. *Miss M, 16, Hertford*

The following are typical negative thoughts collected from blushers:

> People will think I am an awkward, gauche person.

> Now everyone will know I feel so insecure.

> I look so ridiculous, what must they be thinking.

> Where have I gone wrong now?

> I'll never be like other people.

> I feel so silly, stop looking at me.

> Everyone will talk about me because I am blushing.

> I know I'll blush and won't be able to cope.

> I can never say what I think; because of my blushes no one will take me seriously.

We fear a blush happening, think people are noticing, feel foolish and imagine that others view us negatively, which makes us blush even more, as the following two comments illustrate only too clearly.

> I'm always conscious of what other people think of me. I start to go red, and then they know this and I feel as if they are thinking 'What is she blushing for' and that makes me go even redder. *Miss M, 16, London*

> If I even think about my appearance when in public I flush with self-consciousness and then worry madly about my red face. I wonder what people must think of me, and then I worry about going even redder. *Miss E, 25, nurse, Sussex*

But why should other people notice? Why should they view us negatively? Why should it matter? In a blush-inducing situation our thoughts are often rather negative; it is these thoughts that create unpleasant feelings. It is not other people who are saying you are foolish, *it is you!* Even if others do notice your blushes and actually ask: 'Why are you blushing?' they are not telling you that you look silly or incompetent. And if they are actually trying to show you up why should you let them? – they are the ones who should be made to feel foolish not you.

It is important to recognize the part played by negative and sometimes automatic ways of thinking in making yourself feel bad about blushing. This is the first step in learning to deal with worrying thoughts. In order to help yourself to recognize the pattern of your thinking you will find it helpful to keep a weekly record of thoughts in blush-inducing situations.

Recording thoughts

The best way to record your thoughts is to write them down as soon as they happen. For each blushing episode record the date and time, the situation you were in when the blush occurred, the severity of your blushing episode, how long your blush lasted and the precise thoughts that went through your mind the moment your blush began. These might take the form of images rather than words but try to describe your thoughts precisely or write them down word for word if possible. In order to help yourself monitor your thoughts you might use a record form such as that shown in Figure 7 (a completed record is given in Figure 9 in Chapter 8 and you may find it useful to refer to that as an example of the sorts of things you might include). Rate the severity of your blush on the following five point scale:

1 = Not particularly severe
2 = Moderately severe
3 = Somewhat severe
4 = Very severe
5 = Extremely severe

Figure 7. Record of thoughts when blushing

Week number _____

Date _____

Day	Date	Situation	Severity (1–5)	Time lasted	Thoughts
Monday		1 2 3			
Tuesday		1 2 3			
Wednesday		1 2 3			
Thursday		1 2 3			
Friday		1 2 3			
Saturday		1 2 3			
Sunday		1 2 3			

It might not be possible to complete your record sheet immediately after a blushing episode has occurred. In this case try to set aside some time each day to keep the record sheet up to date. Run through the episode in your mind trying to record in as much detail as

64

possible the event and the precise thoughts you had at that moment. It is important to keep accurate and consistent records as these will be useful for identifying and characterizing your pattern of thinking and to provide the basis for instituting change.

Patterns of thinking

From the thoughts you have recorded and from your general way of thinking about yourself, your blushing and your attempts to cope, it is possible to recognize a number of different aspects to negative thoughts. Once you have identified your pattern of thinking the next step is to evaluate how realistic your thoughts are (this can be achieved by asking yourself questions as suggested below); you can then begin to look for more helpful and realistic alternatives.

It is not that you are always wrong about situations; some are clearly hard to deal with. However, focusing on the negative aspects of situations makes them even more difficult to face. It is also not simply a case of looking on the bright side of things. By examining alternative ways of looking at a situation and focusing on ways of dealing with our blushes and our fear of blushing it is possible to gradually feel more in control. First, though, we will examine the way in which blushes can be made worse both by the way we interpret situations and by the things we say to ourselves in those situations.

Overgeneralizing

No one blushes as often or as severely as I do. *Mrs C, 26, secretary, Fife*

I'm forever telling my husband that I'm not good at anything. *Mrs F, 27, Dorset*

I think about blushing all the time. *Mrs R, 25, Scotland*

What is the likelihood that Mrs C blushes more than *everyone* else; that Mrs F is no good at *anything*, or that Mrs R thinks about blushing *all* the time? No matter how severe Mrs C's blushing there will undoubtedly be times when someone else will blush more. No matter how clumsy Mrs F is or how much difficulty she experiences with everyday tasks there will be many things she does well. No matter how much time Mrs R spends thinking about blushing there will be times when something else fills her thoughts. Sometimes we over-generalize the negative side of our thinking – we totally overlook the times we coped with a blush, did not blush, did not think about blushing or succeeded in some other way.

Ask yourself:

- Am I making sweeping assumptions about what will happen when I blush on the basis of one or a few blushing episodes?
- Am I ignoring my strong points and only noticing my weaknesses, one of which, blushing, is placed centre-stage?

Try to replace the negative side of things with a more positive side. Next time you find yourself making a negative prediction about your ability to cope ask yourself 'Have I *always* blushed in this situation in the past? Have people *always* commented? Or, have there been times when I have managed to cope or otherwise managed the situation?' Remind yourself of those times by saying to yourself 'There are times when I do *not* blush; There are things I *am* good at; There are times when *other* people blush more than I do . . .'

Black-or-white thinking

I would love to be a nurse and I have the qualifications to be one – but the thought of working with all those people and knowing I would be red-faced all the time, prevents me from doing so. *Mrs R, 25, East Kilbride*

I am currently unemployed – blushing has prevented me from getting a job. How can I face people with a constant red face? *Mr C, 24, Newcastle*

Very often we think in all-or-nothing, black-or-white terms instead of recognizing that life is made up of a collection of possibilities. If we do not look, or behave or perform perfectly then we tend to think we have failed completely. One aspect of our appearance, a red face, does not mean that we will not work well, that we will not be liked or that we cannot get on in life. By equating one aspect of our appearance with total failure we are not giving ourselves a chance.

Ask yourself:

- Am I only thinking about the black side of things – that I will constantly blush?
- Am I thinking in all-or-nothing terms such as: I can do it if I do not blush/I cannot do it if I do blush?

Try to replace all-or-nothing words with more in-between words that reflect the fact that everyone has good as well as bad points and successes as well as failures. Next time you find yourself saying you cannot do something because you blush, think of your good points, what you can achieve and what you will miss if you do not give yourself a chance.

Absolutist thoughts

Watch out for the words *must*, *should*, *always*, and *never*:

I had to attend two meetings yesterday; I knew I was in for an ordeal because I always blush. *Mrs J, 31, Wigan*

Because of my blushes I can never enjoy myself. No method for reducing blushing ever works; I've tried them all. *Mrs H, 29, Chester*

Ask yourself:

- Am I overestimating the likelihood that everything will always go wrong; that I will always blush?
- Am I making predictions about what will happen in the future instead of starting afresh and testing out each new situation as it happens?

Try to replace absolute words with relative ones: replace *always* with *sometimes*, *never* with *occasionally*, *must* with *perhaps*. Life is far from absolute. Never mind how problematic something is; there will be occasions when we surprise ourselves. It is interesting that Mrs J referred to above continued her comments by saying:

The meeting actually went very well. I ended up taking some notes and actually doing some talking, which I was shocked at. *Mrs J, 31, Wigan*

Taking action

It is important to carefully examine the way you think. Keep a record, see if you are being logical or rational or if you are overgeneralizing, making black-or-white assumptions or being over harsh on yourself by telling yourself you can never succeed, will always blush and so on. Recognizing this pattern of thinking is the first step towards being able to change. In addition, there are a number of positive steps that you can take in order to institute change. These require practice and hard work and you might find it helpful to set yourself a series of targets to aim for as suggested in Chapter 8. First, though, we will examine the available strategies.

Self-talk

One way of coping with blush-inducing situations is by using positive self-talk or self-instructions. When you know you are likely to be in a difficult, blush-inducing situation or when you are actually blushing change the negative thoughts to positive ones. Instead of thinking 'I will blush', 'Everyone will notice' and 'I will feel foolish', say to yourself: 'I will cope', 'It's not the worst thing that could happen' and even 'If I blush it won't be as bad as I expect'. Remind yourself that *you are in control, you are confronting the problem* and *you can remain in control.*

You will find it helpful to write down your own positive self-talk phrases although you could use two or three of the following:

- *Preparing yourself for a difficult situation:*
  I can cope with it.
  I will not be negative.
  I will think rationally.
  I will not worry; it won't help.
  I will manage the situation.
- *Positive self-talk when blushing:*
  It's not the worst thing that could happen to me.
  This is a good chance for me to practise coping.
  I will just pause and be positive.
  I can handle this challenge.
  I am going to stay and confront this.

Remember to pat yourself on the back every time you do manage a difficult situation, if you confront a situation rather than avoid it or if you stay rather than leave. In fact, *anytime* you have succeeded *in spite* of your fear of blushing, say to yourself 'Well done!' but do not put yourself down on the occasions you don't succeed; you have been doing that for too long.

- *Positive self-talk if you succeed:*
  It's getting better.
  I'm pleased with myself.
  I can do it and I will.
  It's not so bad after all.
  When I control my thoughts I control my blushes.

Redirecting attention

In addition to making use of self-talk you can also use various distraction techniques to cope with blushing. Instead of concentrating on your own thoughts and/or the thoughts of others, concentrate on other mental images or objects. You might find that you can ignore your blushes by concentrating on something pleasant – perhaps the beach scene described in the previous chapter. Alternatively, you might find it helpful to focus all your attention on particular aspects of your environment. One strategy is to monitor carefully the physical appearance of the people around you rather than concentrating on your own thoughts or imagining what other people are thinking. Imagine that you are going to give a friend such a complete description of the person's physical appearance that they would be able to identify that person in a photograph.

- Start by looking at clothing: describe to yourself exactly what he or she is wearing; the colour of the material; the design and shape of the garments.
- Describe to yourself his or her hair: its colour, style and length.
- Watch their body movements: are they moving their hands a lot? Are they smiling? Are they speaking quickly? Do they have an accent? Describe these to yourself.
- If there is more than one person make mental notes about the way they interact: who speaks the most? Can you tell how decisions are made about who should speak and when?
- You might even make a note of other people's skin colours – whether they blush or look hot and bothered.

Work your way through the above points, but whenever you find your thoughts straying towards those that are blush-related change your focus to a new aspect. Concentrate, and do not let your thoughts about blushing win.

The 'what-if' approach

After analysing your pattern of thinking, making use of self-talk techniques and redirecting your attention you will no doubt find that instances of blushing gradually decrease along with your concerns about blushing. But *what if* the worst possible thing *did* happen and you blushed without feeling you could control it?

> One example of how my blushes affect me is Parents' evenings. I tend to worry all day at the prospect of meeting parents, knowing that I am going to blush. I keep thinking wouldn't it be terrible if I went red when talking to a parent; they would think I was embarrassed by what had been said. *Mrs D, 27, teacher, Glamorgan*

Ask yourself: *'What if* the worst possible thing were to come true and I blushed?' No doubt your first reaction to this question would be 'It would be awful! I would look so stupid!' But look at this reaction carefully: is it overly negative? Think whether you would blush *all* the time, whether you would be *completely* incapacitated by blushing and whether people would notice *only* your blushes and *nothing else* about you. Now think of the alternative possibilities: other people may not even notice, and even if they do, will they really care? Ask yourself: 'So what if some people do think I look silly? Not everyone will, so what does it matter what some people think?' At the moment there is one aspect of your appearance that dominates your life – blushing – and you think of yourself as a blusher. But people notice many other things about you, they notice your clothes, your hair, your manner – all the aspects of appearance suggested above for you to monitor in other people. We can still be competent and likeable even if we blush; it is only one aspect of our appearance. Even if other people seek to comment on our blushing our first reaction is to feel negative about ourselves and not about the other person.

Redirecting blame

One peculiar aspect of blushing and embarrassment is that comments by other people about our blushing make us blush even more, so we feel more embarrassed. Our worst fears have been confirmed: 'Other people have noticed, they are wondering why I am blushing and think I look silly.' The last thing we wish to do is to draw attention to ourselves and yet that is just what our blushes have succeeded in doing.

> Blushing first bothered me at school when all my classmates would say: 'You've gone red!' or 'What are you blushing for?' That always made matters worse. Even now people will comment and ask me what the matter is, which makes me feel terrible. *Mr J, 31, Wigan*

> I used to work in a factory with 500 men whose comments would make me blush terribly. I know they didn't mean to be cruel and they probably liked me for it but after they'd gone I'd be in the toilets crying my eyes out. The other nurses would say: 'Ahh, she's blushing' or 'What are you blushing for?' which made me feel even worse. *Mrs T, 40, factory-based nurse, Yorkshire*

Not only do we feel bad because we are blushing but we also feel bad about someone else's comments. We are accepting responsibility for the situation even though someone else has made it worse! It is *others* who are at fault, who are silly or insensitive. We can hold our head high and not feel that we are to blame. Use self-talk phrases such as: 'It is not me who has behaved badly'; 'It is not me who looks foolish'; 'I am sensitive, they are insensitive', and so on.

With hard work and regular practice blushing will not be such a central feature of your life. As you begin to put the various strategies into action so you will gradually feel much more confident.

> Once you feel more in control of your thoughts you become less concerned with what others are thinking. I have gradually felt more in control of my blushing and that things are really not so bad. As I feel more in control so my confidence is slowly but surely beginning to grow. *Mrs T*

Further steps to building your confidence are described in the next chapter. These can be added to the relaxation and thought redirecting and re-evaluating strategies already described so that you can gradually become more and more adept at tackling difficult situations. Remember, though, that practice and perseverance are essential – and that you can get there in the end!

7

Developing confidence

Remember from Chapter 3 that self-consciousness is related to a tendency to focus on our own thoughts and feelings, dwelling on what others might think of us. This, together with the common fear that other people will not take us seriously if we blush, can lead to a general lack of confidence in our ability to cope in social situations. By learning the exercises and tasks described in Chapters 5 and 6, and gradually putting them into practice in difficult situations, you have taken the first important steps towards rebuilding your confidence. This chapter examines the vicious circle of blushing/lack of self-confidence in more detail and describes the additional steps you can take to develop confidence.

The vicious circle: blushing/lack of self-confidence

Every time we face a new situation we are inevitably faced with a certain amount of trepidation and uncertainty. If we start a new job we will probably tread carefully until we find out the rules of the organization; if we meet someone new we will no doubt talk about relatively superficial things so that we can establish some kind of baseline for our new friendship. Because of their novelty such situations present challenges. Some people seem to relish the challenge, others would rather avoid them due to the anxiety they cause. When faced with the unknown there is an increased likelihood that we will do something wrong. The more self-conscious we are, the more concerned we will be at this increased chance of making errors. This very concern will lead to a certain amount of anxiety in new situations and a lack of confidence in our ability to cope. When we are overconcerned about blushing in social situations every social encounter is like a new event causing trepidation and uncertainty. Blushing and lack of self-confidence then build up, as the following comments illustrate.

I've always blushed but the problem seemed to get worse when I went to university to study law. Blushing shattered my confidence and interfered with my work so that the more I learned the less confidence I had. Then because of my uncertainty I would blush with embarrassment. *Miss P, 31, barrister, Norwich*

When I was at school I wanted to be popular like my class mates but never had any confidence in myself as my blushing always got in the way. *Mr G, 25, Birmingham*

Do I blush because I'm not confident or do I lack confidence because I blush? The more confident and secure I feel, the less it seems to happen. For example, I am blushing more at the moment because I've started a new job. *Miss C, 29, London*

The vicious circle of self-consciousness, blushing and lack of self-confidence is illustrated in Figure 8.

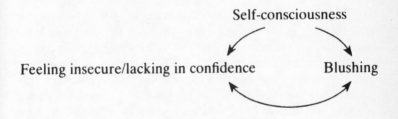

Figure 8. The vicious circle of blushing/lack of self-confidence

Once our blushes have let us down we expect to fail again and again until our confidence is totally sapped. This process can sometimes be set in train by our early learning experiences. If we are constantly criticized we quickly learn that nothing we do seems to be right; if we are constantly told that someone else is better than we are we tend to allow them to be better even to the extent that we put ourselves down.

When I was young my mother was always very critical of everything I did and told me what I should or should not do. She is an absolute perfectionist and I am sure I have had this fear of inadequacy instilled in me from infancy. *Mrs B, East Sussex*

My father always made me feel that men were somehow better than women. Until I was 14 I went to an all-girls school where I thrived and was in the top class. We then amalgamated schools with the local boys' and I dropped down the class. I know I was afraid of looking clever or obvious in front of them. *Mrs G, London*

However, it is possible to reverse the cycle, gradually increasing self-confidence and decreasing concern with blushing.

I feel that if I could stop blushing it would enhance my self-confidence a great deal. That would be lovely! *Mrs H, 33, Bedfordshire*

By possessing the skills (i.e. the exercises and tasks described in Chapters 5 and 6) to cope with blushing you have taken a major step in reversing the cycle. You will not necessarily stop blushing but you will have techniques available for controlling your blushes and your fear of blushing; the fact you are now able to control the situation rather than allowing your fear of blushing to be in control means that your confidence will steadily grow. To encourage this process there are a number of additional steps you can take which are described below. These can be broadly grouped into three categories and involve being positive about yourself, being positive about others' reactions and beginning to control your life.

Steps towards building self-confidence

Be positive about yourself

We are often inclined to notice our bad points and remember our mistakes, often overlooking our good points and forgetting our achievements. Be more positive about yourself – if you don't emphasize your strong points no one else will!

- *Recognize your strengths and weaknesses.* Make a list of your good points and begin to emphasize these; everyone has good as well as bad points. Often, though, we think of our weaknesses first, as the following comment illustrates:

My blushing problem seems worse because basically I have low self-esteem, I am too sensitive and 'thin-skinned', full of self-doubt and lacking in confidence. Yet in spite of this I have had several responsible jobs and worked for a few years as a counsellor for the Samaritans. *Mrs T, 40, Cleveland*

Begin to place your strengths and achievements above points you see as weaknesses. In fact, some things we perceive as weaknesses may be seen by others as strengths! In Mrs T's case, for example, her sensitivity – which she lists as a weakness – may have enabled her to obtain work as a counsellor for the Samaritans who saw it as a strength.

- *Blushing is only one aspect of you that other people might notice.* Build on other aspects of yourself and avoid concentrating on your blushes (even if other people notice they may not care!). Mrs R, for example, comments:

  Blushing has affected my whole life; it has stopped me from doing things. I find I cannot form very close relationships because I feel very stupid about my colouring-up. I also feel I might frighten people away because I blush so much. *Mrs R*

Anyone who dislikes us because we blush is really not worth knowing anyway. If you are friendly, helpful and understanding many people will like you whether you blush or not.

- *Recognize when you have achieved something.* Learn to pat yourself on the back; do not look for failure or the negative side of your achievements. Consider the following comment from Mrs B:

  My blushing has not stopped me from joining evening classes, but I just hope that I can get away with being inconspicuous because as soon as anyone speaks I will blush. *Mrs B*

By emphasizing her fear that she will blush Mrs B is diminishing her achievements; any '*But . . .*' should be followed by 'I will achieve more tomorrow' and not by 'I did not really achieve anything anyway'.

Be positive about others' reactions

We tend to assume that because we are aware of certain aspects of ourselves that we consider to be weaknesses then other people will inevitably notice them as well. But we are sensitized to these aspects of ourselves; other people are much less aware of us than we might think.

- *Do not assume that you are always the centre of attention.* Most people are all too often wrapped in their own thoughts concerned about something else altogether. Mrs L comments that:

  When I go to the canteen there are always one or two women there who look at me when I come in and at the same time are laughing. The first thing I think is why are they laughing at me, which makes me blush. I never think that they might be laughing at something else. *Mrs L, Hertfordshire*

  In fact it is most likely that they were laughing at something else. People often do not pay us the amount of attention we imagine they do; think how difficult it is to attract someone's attention when you actually want to!

- *Do not put thoughts into other people's heads.* Don't assume you know what people are thinking – you may not be correct. The following comment by Mrs F illustrates this point:

  I am aware of my blushing being much worse when I am speaking to authority figures – even though they are friendly towards me. I know they feel sorry for me when I go beetroot the moment they approach. *Mrs F, Fife*

  Other people may well be thinking something totally different about Mrs F – in fact they may not be thinking of her at all; they may be thinking about their work, a forthcoming meeting, or any manner of alternatives.

- *Do not always view other people's comments or reactions in a negative light.* Even if people do make remarks, avoid blaming yourself for other's comments. Mrs R again states:

Blushing has affected my confidence in settling down in jobs. I had a job in a factory where I am sure I could have got on well, but because people were always commenting on how I blushed, I felt I had to leave because I let their comments get to me so much I started making silly mistakes. *Mrs R*

Other people should have better things to do – it is their failure when they try to make you feel small, not yours. As Miss M comments:

I remind myself that it's not me who bothers about my blushing; it's other people. In the past when I went red and they would comment it would make me go red even more – that was what made me feel embarrassed. Now I tell myself it's their problem not mine. *Miss M, London*

* *Try not to worry about the odd emotional bruising you might take.* Never mind the knocks, you can still bounce back; in fact you are probably tougher than you think. We may feel like Mrs H, who comments:

If I go out for a drink and there are a few of us chatting I will never say a word because everyone would watch me and I would blush. So if I have a view or want to say something I have to keep it bottled up inside and then I get annoyed with myself because I know I should have said something. *Mrs H, St Albans*

Go ahead and say what you think, people will respect you for it; and even if they dismiss your view or fail to take you seriously, try again and again. You may fail sometimes but you will succeed sometimes as well; as your success grows your confidence will grow as well.

* *Allow yourself to accept compliments.* If other people praise you it is because they recognize something good about you. Even if you don't allow yourself to accept your good points, allow others to recognize them. Mrs G comments:

I find myself getting hot and bothered over nothing; if someone pays me a compliment, on my hair for instance, where other

women might say 'Thank you very much', I blush and say
something to run myself down, like, 'Oh! there's nothing to it
really', or I am just off-hand which must make me seem rude.
Mrs G, 36, London

Even if you do blush others may see it positively rather than
negatively: blushing when praised is often seen as a sign of modesty
(i.e. 'I may be good but not *that* good!')

Control your life

Perhaps the most important aspect of learning relaxation and
distraction techniques is that they give you the chance to be in
control of your own reactions. You now have the ability to control
your blushes and your fear of blushing. As you start to be more in
control, you will start to build and control your life in other ways as
well. The more you do and the more you succeed, so the more your
confidence will grow.

• *Set yourself both short-term and long-term goals.* This is in order
  to establish a pattern to your life over which you are exerting
  control. Make sure these are realistic aims and not impossible
  targets; each short-term goal should be difficult but manageable –
  the sort of thing you can achieve on a good day although it is hard
  work. Build up gradually and give yourself a suitable reward for
  each step you take, perhaps treating yourself to a special present.
  Mrs M, in describing how blushing has affected her life, gives a
  list of possible targets to aim towards:

  I can't begin to tell you all the times blushing has stopped me
  from doing things I really wanted to do; how many parties,
  weddings and such like I have missed by making an excuse at
  the last minute. I don't want to live like this; I want to lead a
  normal life. I want to attend my children's school functions
  without worrying about it for weeks beforehand, I want to go to
  neighbours' clothes parties, coffee mornings and so on, which I
  can't do at the moment. *Mrs M*

One thing for Mrs M to do would be to start with small
gatherings, perhaps with one or two people she knows well,
building up gradually to bigger and more important events. You

might construct your own hierarchy of things you want to achieve. It does not matter how many small steps there are. Before taking each step prepare yourself by relaxing and clearing your thoughts.

- *Remember that you are not a passive object that things just happen to.* Each of us is a unique individual who can make things happen for ourself. We may feel like Mr P, who comments:

Blushing is restraining my performance at work and future opportunities. I want to express myself fully in life but I am held back because of the fear of blushing, and often I just want to hide and avoid situations. *Mr P, 31, West Midlands*

It takes a great deal of hard work but we can change our entire lives if we really put our minds to it. Don't let life pass you by. As Mrs B says:

I tell myself to stop envying other people and to accept myself the way I am. If I do not accept myself no one else will. I am striving to cope with my blushing – I keep repeating to myself 'I will win the battle one day'. *Mrs B, Chesterfield*

8
Putting the package together and monitoring change

The preceding seven chapters can be grouped broadly into three sections: explanation (Chapters 1 and 2 and part of Chapter 3), assessment (part of Chapter 3 and Chapter 4), and strategies for change (Chapters 5, 6 and 7). Each of these sections offers information about blushing or techniques for coping with blushing, which together constitute an overall package for instituting change. There are two aims of this chapter: first, to summarize briefly and pinpoint the key components of the overall package in order to answer the question: How can I cope with blushing? Second, to stress the need for keeping a weekly record of blushing in order to monitor change while putting coping strategies into practice.

Key points for learning to cope with blushing

There are 14 key points listed below that summarize the psychological processes involved in chronic blushing and the strategies for promoting change. You might like to refer back to this from time to time as a way of reminding yourself of key elements of the programme.

1 *Understanding is the first step towards coping.* It is important to recognize that blushing involves not only a bodily response but a particular pattern of thoughts which increases concern about blushing. Recognizing this forms the background to promoting change.
2 *Becoming less concerned with your own behaviour and others' reactions will decrease concern with blushing.* Self-consciousness is related to a tendency to worry about blushing; the more concerned we are about others' reactions the more flustered we will become and the more we will blush or imagine we are blushing. Altering the tendency to focus on our own thoughts and actions and on what others might think of us is central to dealing with chronic blushing.

3 *Blushing is difficult to hide but there are effective strategies for coping with it.* Blushing cannot be 'cured' with physical remedies although many people try medication to dampen reactions, or resort to surgery in the hope of eliminating blushing altogether; others may use creams and clothes to cover blushes. The answer lies within you and the amount you are prepared to practise strategies to enable you to control your life.

4 *Knowing how we react allows us to select appropriate strategies for promoting change.* Recognizing that we do not all react in the same way and that the interaction of thoughts and bodily reactions will be different for different people allows us to select the strategy to meet our individual needs.

5 *Learn to relax, it will help you to be calmer.* Like any other skill learning to relax takes a great deal of practice. But persevere, it will not only allow you to be generally calmer it will also help you to calm down in situations in which you think you might blush.

6 *Calming images can be used as a place to retreat to in your mind.* When practising relaxation make use of calming images to deepen your state of relaxation. Use the same image each time you practise relaxation. Eventually even under very distressing blush inducing circumstances you will be able to use your calming image as a way of regaining calm control.

7 *Recognize the part played by negative and sometimes automatic ways of thinking in making yourself feel bad about the prospect of blushing.* Keep a record of your thoughts associated with blushing to identify and characterize your pattern of thinking – they provide the basis for instituting change.

8 *How realistic are your thoughts? Look for more helpful and realistic alternatives.* Do you tend to focus on the negative side of the situation, always thinking that something will go wrong? Remember that it is not other people who are telling you you look silly or incompetent – it is you! It is your own thoughts that create unpleasant feelings; work on changing them.

9 *Avoid overgeneralizing from one situation to another.* Each situation is new and presents a different set of challenges – there will undoubtedly be times when you succeed, when you cope with blushing, do not blush or do not think about blushing. Recognize these occasions and praise yourself accordingly.

10 *Avoid thinking in all-or-nothing or absolutist terms.* Life is made

up of a collection of possibilities, nothing is ever absolute. Start afresh and test out each situation as it happens.

11 *Positive self-talk can help.* When in difficult situations remind yourself that you are in control, you are confronting the problem and can remain in control. Pat yourself on the back every time you succeed in spite of your fear of blushing.

12 *Distraction techniques can be used to cope with blushing.* Instead of concentrating on your own thoughts and/or imagined thoughts of others concentrate on other mental images or objects, or carefully monitor the appearance of people around you. Build a complete mental picture of them by noting their clothes, hair, movements and so on.

13 *Be positive about yourself and others' reactions.* Recognize your strengths and that blushing is only one aspect of you that other people might notice. Avoid putting thoughts into other people's heads and do not feel that you are responsible for any comments they might make.

14 *Take control of your life.* Set yourself both short-term and long-term goals and work towards changing your life. Practise relaxation and distracting techniques and use them in your daily life. You can cope but you will need to keep working at it.

Monitoring change

You have already been asked in Chapter 5 to keep a record of daily relaxation practice and in Chapter 6 to keep a record of thoughts when blushing. Each serves a slightly different purpose. The record of daily relaxation practice is suggested primarily as a way in which you can help yourself to keep to a particular schedule – a way of encouraging a habit of relaxation practice – although it also provides a way of assessing changes in feelings of tension or relaxation as a result of practising the exercises. The record of thoughts when blushing is suggested primarily as a way of identifying and characterizing your pattern of thinking in order to provide a basis for instituting change. Keeping a weekly record of thoughts and events associated with blushing also serves another very important function – it is a way of monitoring change while putting coping strategies into practice.

Figure 7 in Chapter 6 provides a useful chart for using on a weekly basis to monitor blushing. As well as providing a record of the situations in which blushing occurs and thoughts when blushing it also enables us to record three further central aspects of blushing:

1 Blushing frequency – the number of occasions a blush is recorded.
2 Blushing intensity – the average intensity rating for all blushing episodes in each week.
3 Blushing duration – the average length of time that a blush lasted in each week.

The example given in Figure 9 is from the sixth week of records kept by Mrs O, a 51-year-old medical secretary whom I saw in my clinic.

Figure 9. Example from a record of blushing episodes

Week number six, beginning 27th February

Day	Date	Situation	Severity (1–5)	Time lasted	Thoughts
Monday	27th	1 Reception area: Praised by doctor for getting work done	4	7 min	I wish she hadn't singled me out
Tuesday	28th	1 Reception area: Doctor telling me about a funeral – everyone can hear	3	4½ min	What will the patients think?
		2 Small shop: At checkout I've put the wrong thing in my basket and have to change it	5	25 min	Everyone is looking at me – how silly I must look
Wednesday	1st	1 Bus full of people: An acquaintance called out to me	5	15 min	Everyone is looking at me
		2 Reception area: A patient keeps talking to me while I'm working	3	6 min	Why does he have to keep talking to me?

Thursday	2nd	1 Bus full of people: I stood up to let a young mother with a baby sit down – another woman said how good it was of me	5	10 min	Everyone is looking – how foolish I must look for blushing
Friday	3rd	1 Small clothes shop: Someone suddenly asked me the time	2	$\frac{1}{2}$ min	I was taken by surprise and wondered what she must think of me
		2 Hairdresser's: Hot under the hairdryer while the stylist is talking to me	3	2 min	I hope she realizes it is the heat making me blush
		3 Restaurant with a colleague of my husband and colleague's wife: she asked me what my job was	3	4 min	I've gone pink how stupid
Saturday	4th	1 Supermarket: Stranger asked me the price of something in my basket	2	1 min	What must she think of me
		2 Restaurant: Left gloves behind – waiter shouted after us	4	2 min	Everyone is looking
Sunday	5th	At home all day – nothing to record			

From Mrs O's record we can work out the frequency, average intensity and average severity of her blushes for the sixth week of her diary. The frequency (total number of incidents in the week) was 1 on Monday the 27th plus 2 on Tuesday 28th plus 2 on Wednesday 1st and so on, giving a total of 11 for that week. The average severity is calculated by adding up all the severity ratings (i.e. 4 + 3 + 5 + 5 + 3 and so on), which gives a total of 39 and dividing this by the frequency (i.e. the number of incidents in the week), which was

11 in that week. Thus the average severity (39 divided by 11) is approximately $3\frac{1}{2}$. The average duration is calculated by adding up the time each blush lasted (i.e. 7 minutes + $4\frac{1}{2}$ minutes + 25 minutes and so on) giving a total of 77 minutes for that week and dividing this by the frequency (i.e. 11). Thus the average duration (77 divided by 11) is 7.

We have already seen in Chapter 6 that the record for thoughts when blushing can be used to identify particular patterns of thinking. The situations in which blushes occur can be used in exactly the same way. For example, in Mrs O's case all the situations involve someone speaking to her, often unexpectedly (except for incident 2 on Tuesday which involves being singled out by a mistake). Identifying the situations that cause us most difficulty can help target coping attempts. Because of the unexpected element in the majority of situations described by Mrs O, she found carefully rehearsed distraction techniques to be most helpful in keeping her thoughts away from her blushes.

But why is monitoring change important? It's main importance lies in the continuous and visible record that it provides. Mrs O, for example, recorded figures of 8 for frequency; $2\frac{1}{2}$ for severity and 5 for duration during week 10 and 6 for frequency, 2 for severity and 4 for duration in week 12. The decrease in each of these numbers continued in subsequent weeks although the decline was not smooth – Mrs O had a number of bad weeks. By looking back over her record and reminding herself of her achievements Mrs O was more able to brush off the bad weeks. It helped her to be able to see in black and white that she was actually getting somewhere.

Keeping a detailed record is important, therefore, for two reasons: first, it will help you to gain a clearer understanding of your blushing (the situations giving rise to blushes and the thoughts associated with blushing), and second, it will provide you with a continuous record of change which can be rewarding in its own right. Remember, though, that no amount of record-keeping will work without continuous practice of strategies for promoting change, but it is a battle that can be won.

I look at my blushing as an enemy so that I can fight it – I make myself think positively, I will myself to keep calm. If I manage to keep going through my blushes it seems that no one appears to notice them. I'm gradually building my confidence – it seems like a long, hard struggle, but it is a fight that I am determined to win. *Mrs C, Oxfordshire.*

Blushing: A personal account

You now know what you can do to cope with fear of blushing. The strategies for coping have been described in some detail and it is now up to you to put them into practice. Remember that with practice and perseverance you will gradually start to see the light at the end of the tunnel. But practice and perseverance are essential. Do not expect a miracle cure or overnight change; you may well have suffered for many years so that your present way of reacting and your current image of yourself have had a long time to become established. Luckily, it does not take the same amount of time to alter this established pattern but, inevitably, it does take time and a lot of hard work. Fear of blushing can have a debilitating effect but do not let it rule your life – fight back and put yourself in control.

In writing this book I have illustrated various points with comments from sufferers and you no doubt recognize many of these aspects in yourself. Many people have made the point in their letters that it helps just to know that they are not alone and that many others also suffer agonies from their fear of blushing. We really have no idea how many people suffer nor the real extent of their suffering – the hundreds of people who have written to me no doubt represent the tip of the iceberg. But no matter how much you have suffered it is possible to change. I would like to end this book by allowing one of the long-term sufferers I have seen in my clinic to put into words the distress occasioned by fear of blushing. This account illustrates many of the points made in this book: the disruption to life caused by fear of blushing, the desperate attempts to cover up the blushes and, finally, the recognition that it is possible to learn to control blushes and fear of blushing. I will leave the final words to Mrs T, a 38-year-old teacher from Kent:

I am in the process of confronting a problem that has haunted me for the last 25 years. It is not life-threatening, it does not involve the use of drugs or other harmful substances, but it is something I find quite shameful and something I view in totally negative terms – seeing it as a pathetic weakness. I *blush*. I can almost recall to the day when I was afflicted – for I do see it as an affliction which has altered the course of my life and by implication the lives of those around me. Until the age of 15 I had been a totally outgoing, enthusiastic member of society. I'd stand on stage and recite a poem, take part in any school production and read out loud in class at the flick of a fly leaf. Then one day it happened. I was suddenly aware of my body, or rather two particular parts of my body, my face and my neck.

Puberty had struck three years before and I'd accepted it as a fact of life (which of course it was), but I must admit nothing could have prepared me for this onslaught. Activities I had relished became a nightmare. Life became quite exhausting, not just because of the physical effects of blushing (heart pounding, nausea, sweating, giddiness, etc.), but the mental gymnastics I would perform each day. I would work out when it would be my turn to read aloud or answer a question. I developed a real horror about succeeding, for success brought praise and recognition – honours I could not cope with. Prize-giving used to make me physically ill, but unfortunately I never fainted. I was always conscious of the dastardly trick my body was playing on me.

I used to devour the women's magazines for helpful advice or, better still, a cure. Every few months I would read how blushing always seems worse than it is. The blusher is always more aware of the problem than those around her/him. Frankly, such platitudes were such rubbish! Those agony aunts had not seen me in action! I could blush for Britain; in fact I could be entered for many different categories for by the age of eighteen my blushing was rapidly becoming an art form. I had almost perfected the full frontal cheek blush, including a rather fetching strip of throbbing red down my nose. There were occasions when the blush would start in one cheek then slowly and gracefully flow across my face to embrace my other cheek in a sisterly bond of redness.

Being a true artiste I was developing another string to my blush, my neck. At first, this part of my anatomy had kept relatively cool, however, obviously inspired by the energy of my cheeks it sprang into action and delightful ribbons of red could be seen to envelope my neck. Like my cheeks, my neck developed the capacity to fire on either side or, in really heated encounters, on both sides leaving a demure strip of whiteness down the line of my throat, thus displaying the glowing redness to its full advantage.

Once blushing had gripped me by the throat I decided that I had to learn to cope with my incapacitating enemy. After I left school my wardrobe consisted mainly of high neck jumpers and scarves. Admittedly the summer proved a problem, but you could always get a chiffon scarf. My sociability declined in proportion to the strength of the sun's rays, thus the warmer the weather the more reticent I became. I could be quite vociferous in the winter under a thick polo-neck and matching scarf but the sun's appearance put a damper on my social activities.

Make-up was a vital part of my camouflage. One marvellous day I read about green make-up which would tone you down. This green masque was applied first, then normal make-up was to be placed on top. Unfortunately, I never quite mastered the art of applying either type of make-up and the result was cheeks that still burned like erotic glow worms, only this time surrounded by a ring of green tinted sludge. It was in this delightful state that I passed four years at university and finally qualified as a teacher. I couldn't believe I had done it; I mean, a blusher of such magnitude prepared to parade herself in front of one of the most cruel and critical sectors of society – children.

By the time I was thirty flushing had taken its toll on my face. The area across my cheeks and nose was a mass of broken veins and rough skin and now I had an obvious physical problem as well as the emotional one that I had been coping with over the years. I decided to approach my doctor and in my best grovelling manner I explained how my skin was not a problem really and that actually I was not a vain person and that maybe he could suggest a cream that might alleviate the soreness and reduce the rash that seemed to be forming under the skin. Rubbing his healing thumbs across my cheeks he suggested that I learn to cover it up and that is how I found myself sitting in a beautician's salon undergoing electrolysis to remove the offending thread veins. After three very painful visits the therapists acknowledged that I was not responding to treatment and the resulting inflammation and bleeding were signs that I must have very sensitive skin. I drove home after that final visit with tears streaming down my burning cheeks. I still bear the scars of that course of treatment and when, four years later, I explained to a consultant dermatologist what I had undergone I saw the man visibly blanch at the thought of needles being stuck into such delicate tissue.

The consultant examined my skin and stated that I had *acne rosacea* – a sort of butterfly rash that affects the cheeks and nose and is usually aggravated by alcohol, hot drinks, spicy foods, etc. I was prescribed antibiotics for a year and it was suggested that a course of beta-blockers might help to calm me down and so reduce the facial flushing. However, the antibiotics caused a moss-like substance to grow on my tongue and the beta-blockers slowed me down so much that my blood seemed very reluctant to flow into my hands and feet and my famous red cheeks appeared to be turning a rather violent shade of purple.

And so, at the age of thirty-eight I decided to accept my weakness and learn to live with it. However, this was easier said than done. I continued to blush in the most ridiculous and unimportant situations, but valiantly I continued to act normally even though my body constantly humiliated me.

It must have been about six months ago that I was reading a Sunday Supplement article about the body and there in black and white was an article about a clinical psychologist who was studying blushing. You would have thought that this information would have sent me hurrying to the telephone to contact this human version of the Holy Grail. Not so. If the article had described him as a neurologist or a dermatologist I might have rushed to place my cheeks in his hands, but the term psychologist sounded alarm bells in my mind – it told me what I had known all along, but never wanted to admit, that the blushing was part of the essential me. All through my life I had wanted blushing to be a physical problem; something to do with my body thermostat or oversensitive nerve endings; an allergy to life or something to do with my bodily functions.

It took me almost a month to compose that first letter to the psychologist. He replied almost by return of post with photo-copies of articles he had written and notes on how to reduce anxiety and stress and most important of all an invitation to consult him if I so wished. I did so wish and my first visit took place in February and the suggested course of five sessions was under way, with him promising me no miracle cure but rather developing within me the ability to redirect and reduce my stress and anxiety. He explained to me how I had to break into the circular reaction I had set up in my body, namely when I am in a stressful situation, I blush, when I blush I panic more because I am blushing, therefore I blush more, and so on, until I turn into a glowing, sweating mass of humanity.

Part of my therapy has been to keep a diary of daily events and how I have reacted to them and to tabulate the degree to which I have blushed, e.g. spoke at staff meeting, 5/5, total blush, neck to eyebrows. I don't expect to stop blushing but perhaps I will learn to live with it with more equanimity. I hope to reduce the anger and humiliation I feel when my body lets me down and sends out what I consider to be totally erroneous signals to those around me, for I am an intelligent, articulate woman who is keenly aware of how trifling her problem might seem but who wants to be allowed to get up on that damned stage just once more.

Useful addresses

The National Phobics Society
Zion Community Resource Centre
339 Stretford Road
Hume
Manchester M15 4ZY
0161 227 9898
www.phobics-society.org.uk

A national registered charity with the aim of promoting awareness, understanding and treatment of all fears and phobias. The society publishes the 'Don't Panic' newsletter which contains lists of therapy and self-help services, details of local groups and contacts, plus information articles. The society also publishes booklets (including one on relaxation training) and fact sheets (including one on blushing).

Triumph Over Phobia (TOP UK)
PO Box 1831
Bath
BA2 4YW
01225 330353
www.triumphoverphobia.com

A registered charity that runs a national network of structured self-help groups for adults suffering from a phobia.

British Association for Behavioural & Cognitive Psychotherapies
The Globe Centre
PO Box 9
Accrington
BB5 0XB
01254 875277
www.babcp.com

A national association that can provide details of cognitive-behavioural therapists listed in your locality.

Further reading

Edelmann, Robert J. (2001), 'Blushing'. In W. R. Crozier and L. E. Alden (eds), *International Handbook of Social Anxiety: Concepts, Research and Interventions Relating to the Self and Shyness*. Chichester: John Wiley & Sons.
This provides an academic review of research relating to all aspects of blushing.

Hansen, Maurice (1987), *E for Additives*. London: Thorsons.

Markway, B. G., C. N. Carmin, C. A. Pollard & T. Flynn (1992), *Dying of Embarrassment: Help for Social Anxiety & Phobia*. Oakland CA: New Harbinger.

Rapee, R. (2001), *Overcoming Shyness and Social Phobia: A Step-by-Step Guide*. Horthvale NJ: Jason Aronson Publishers.

Schneier, F. R. & L. A. Welkowitz (1996), *The Hidden Face of Shyness*. Morrow/Avon (a US imprint of HarperCollins Book group).

Index